Belongs To: ____________________

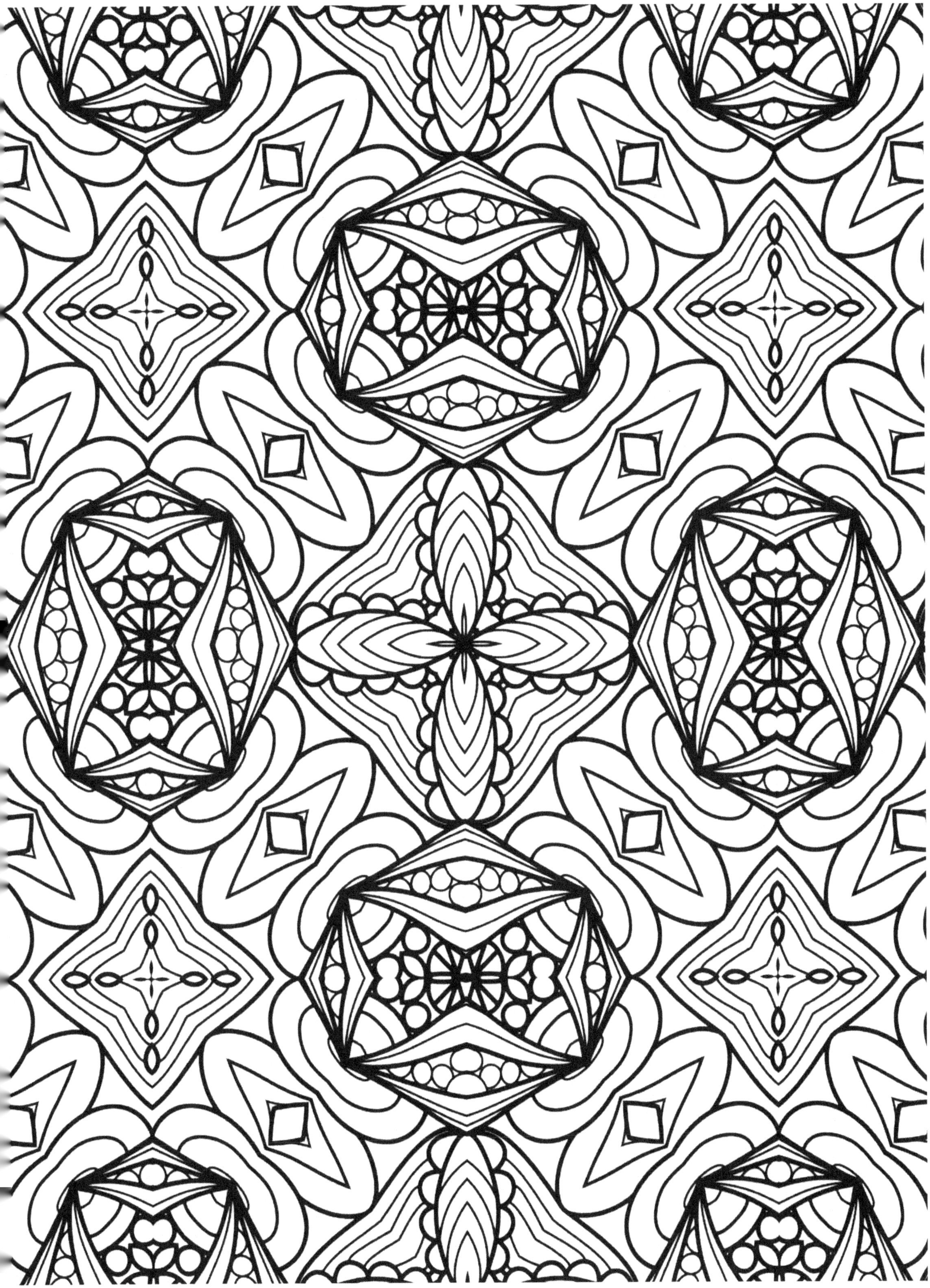

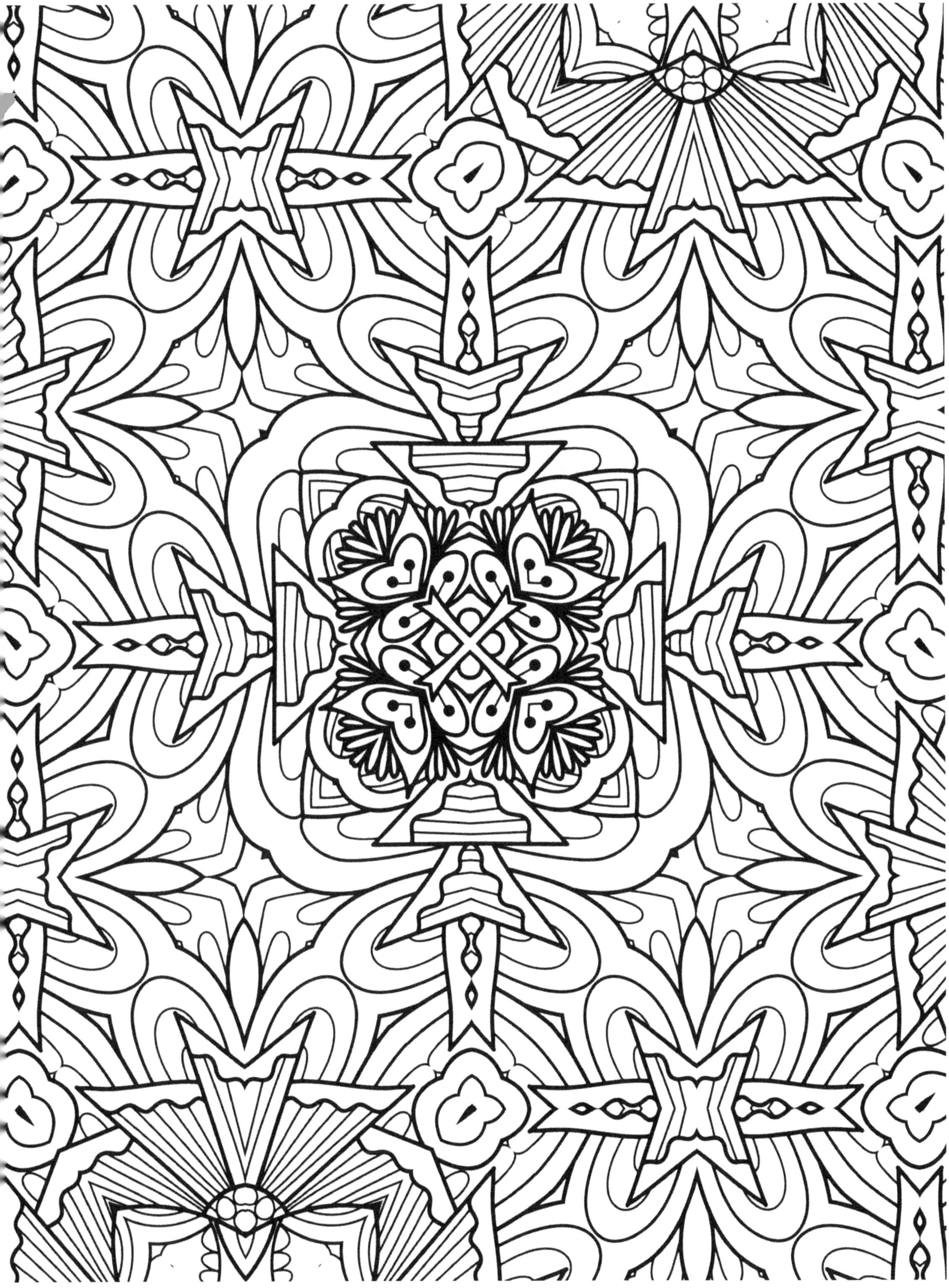

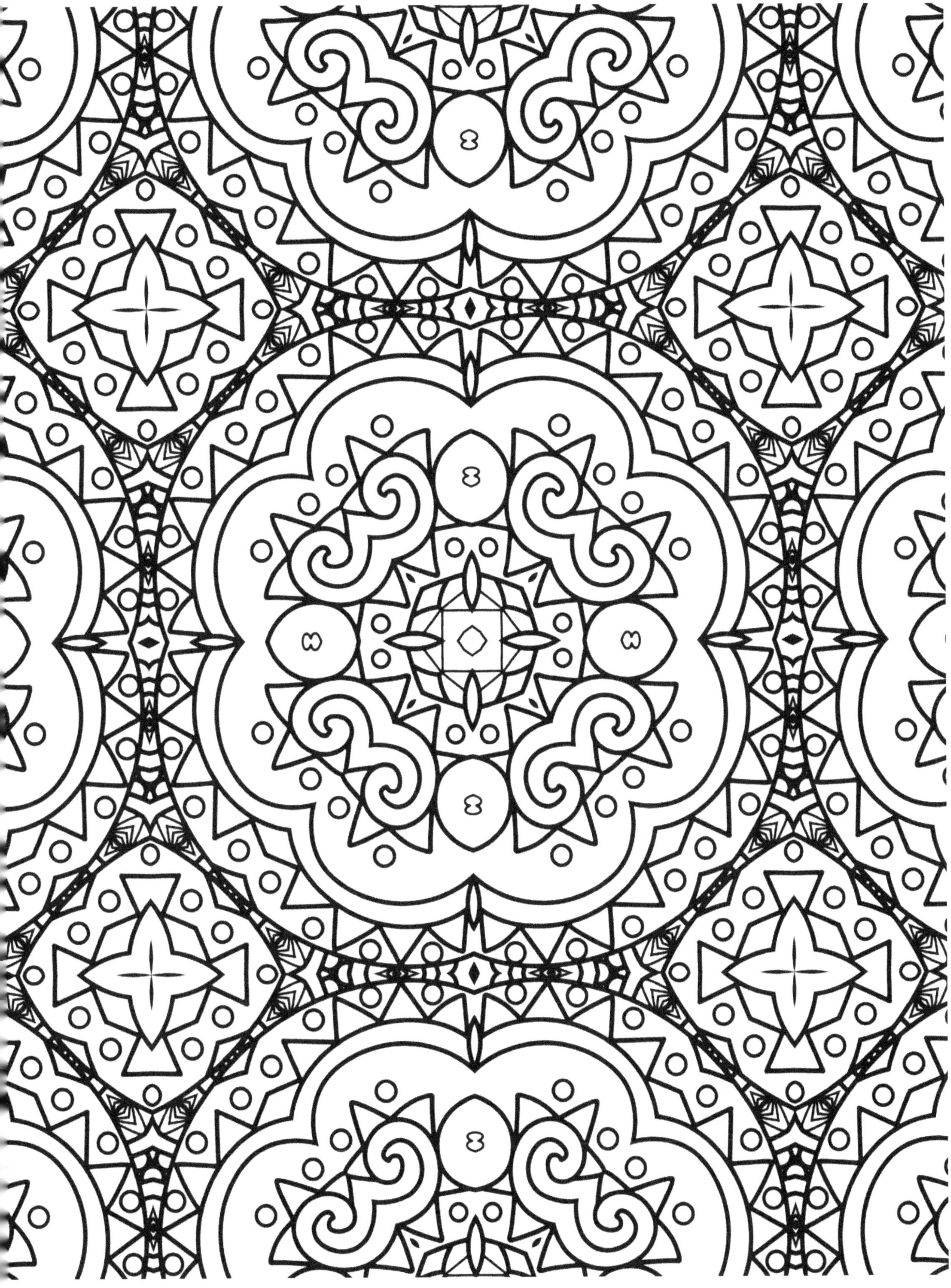

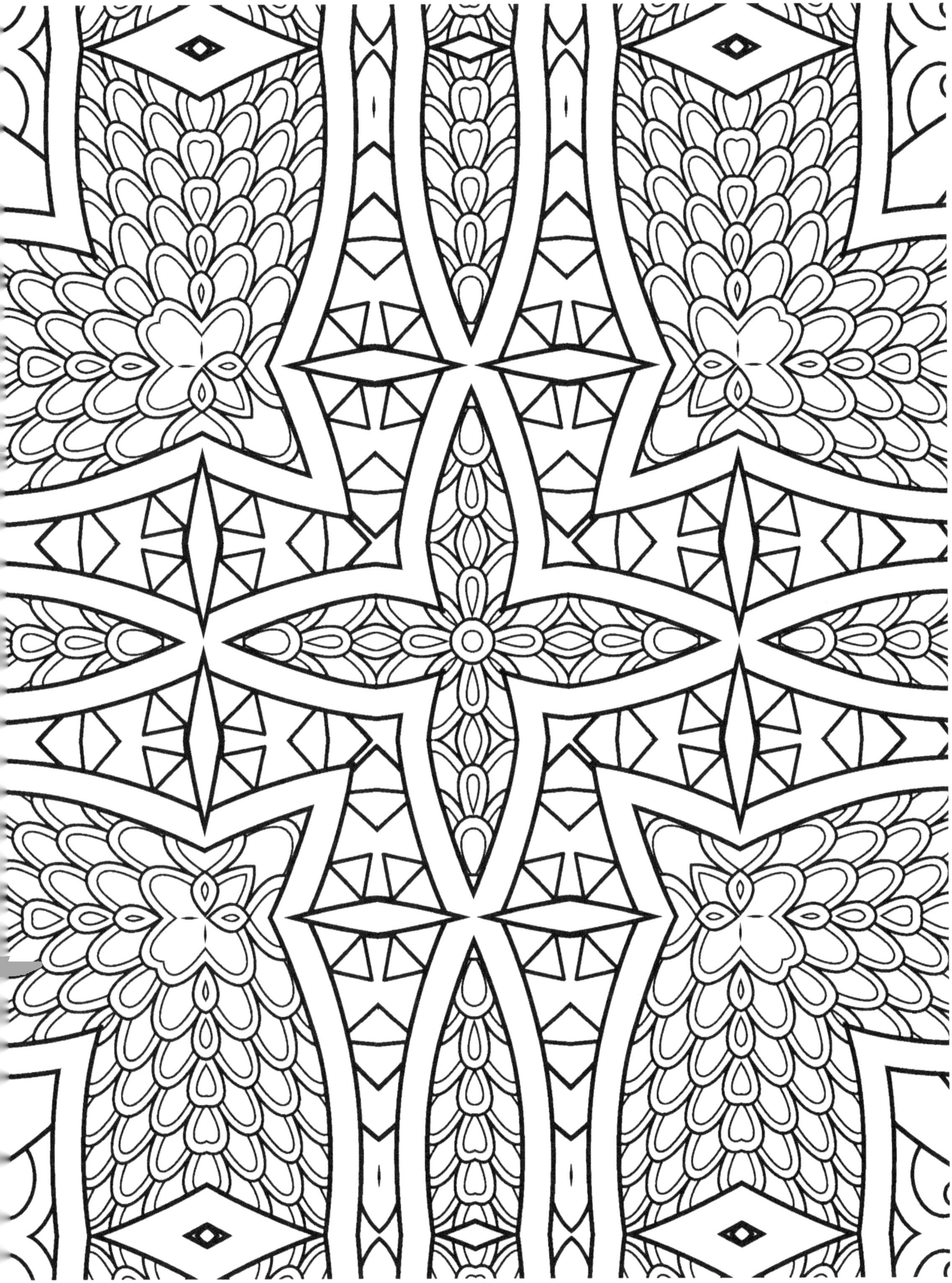

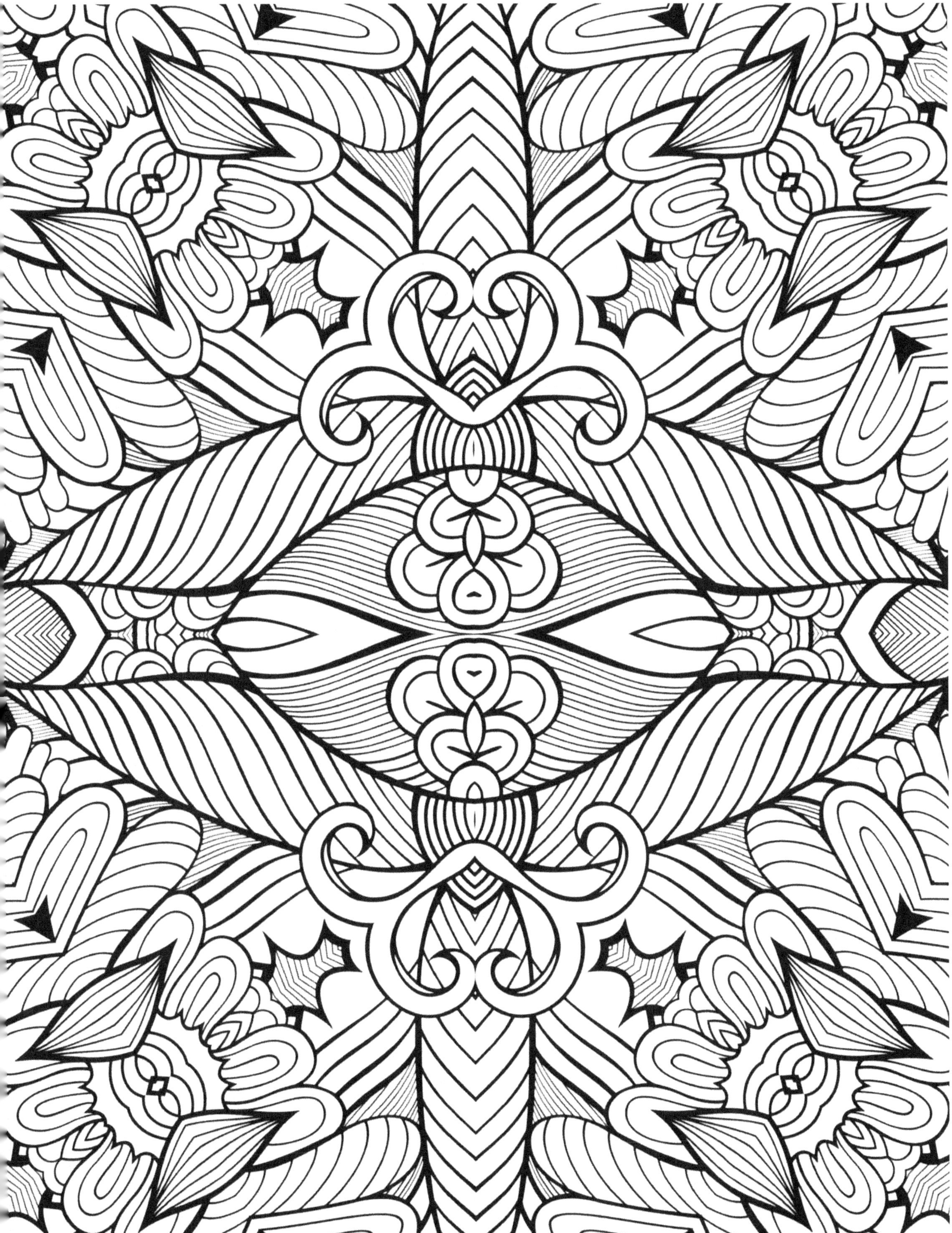

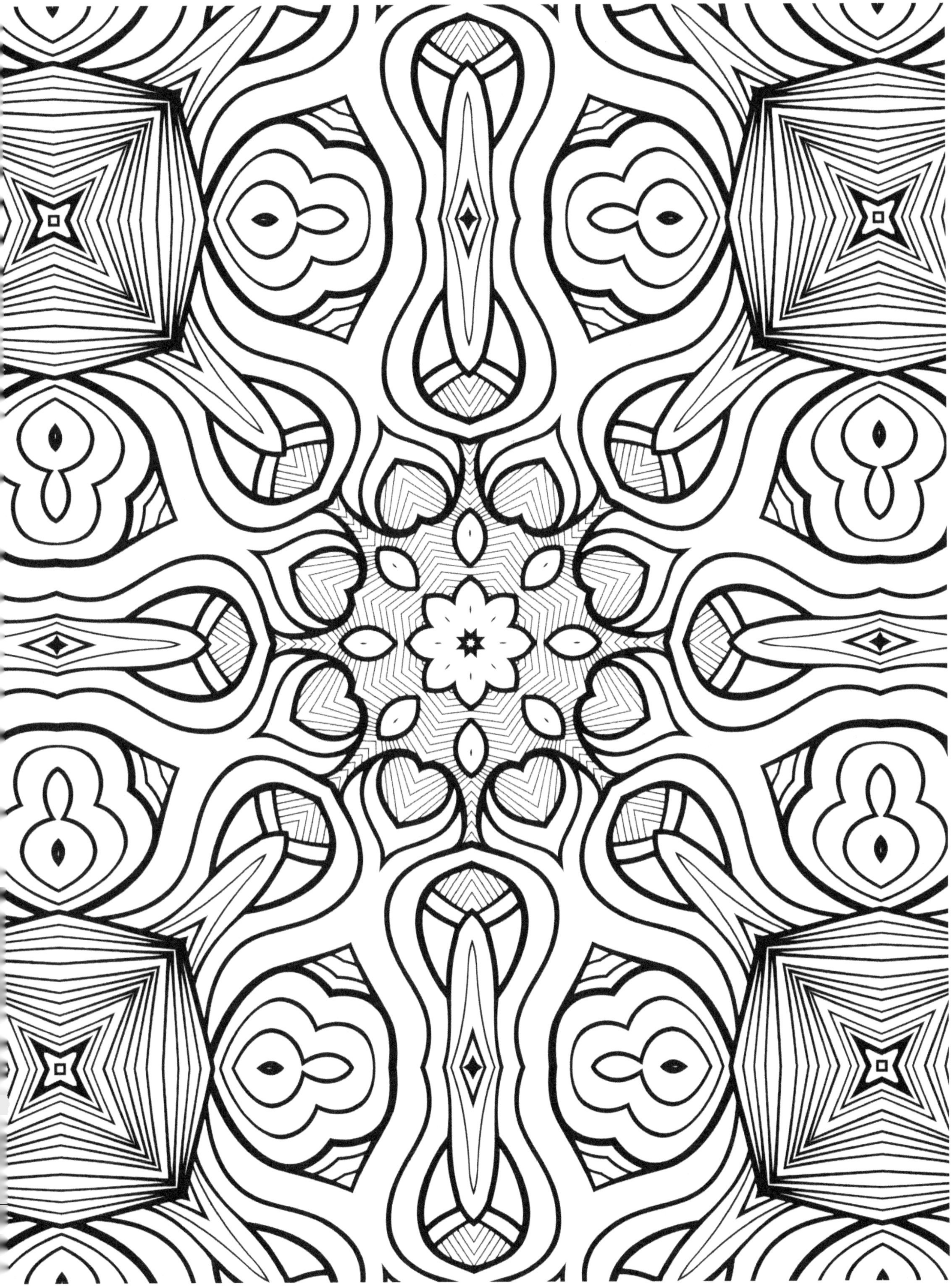

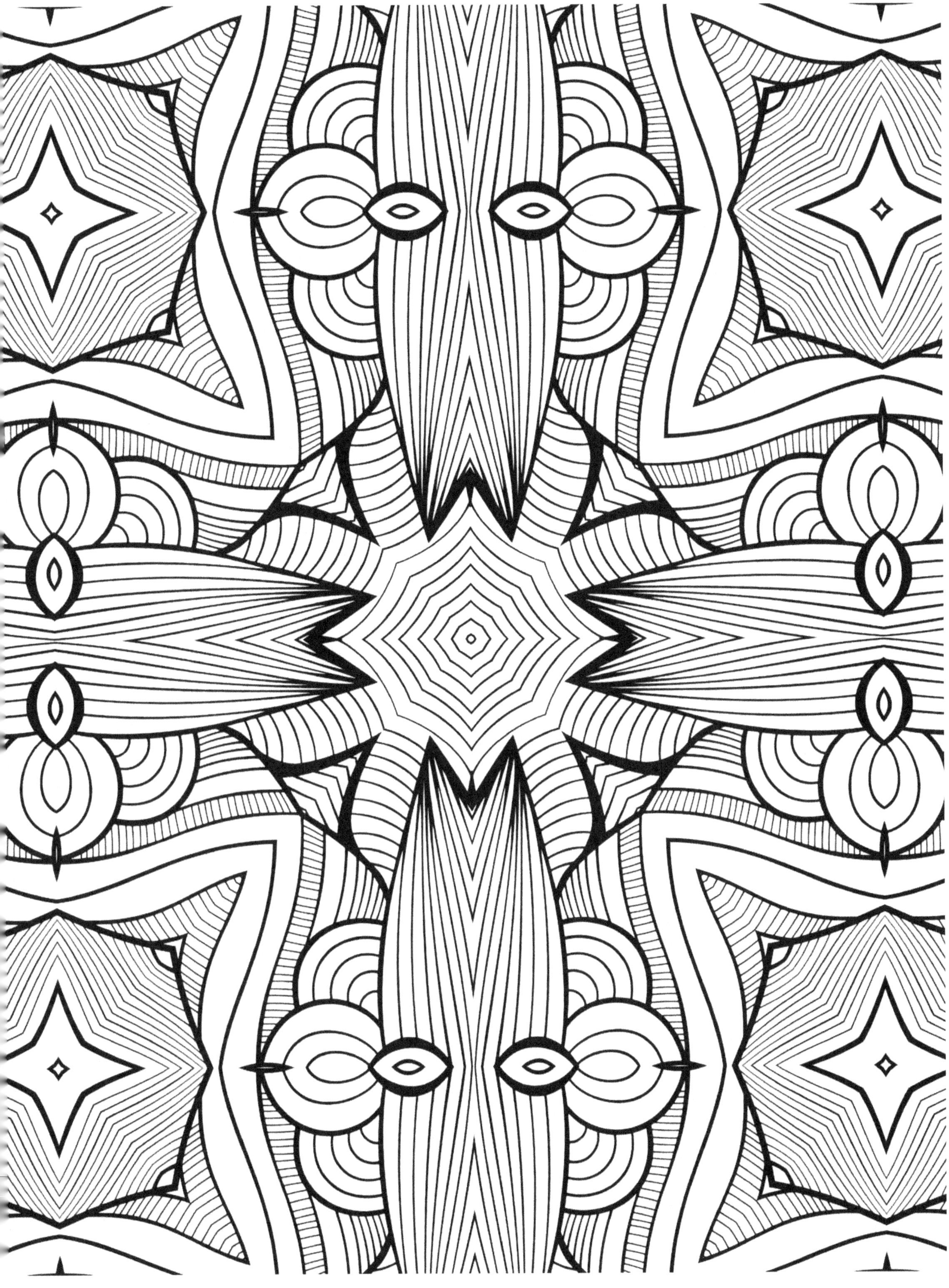

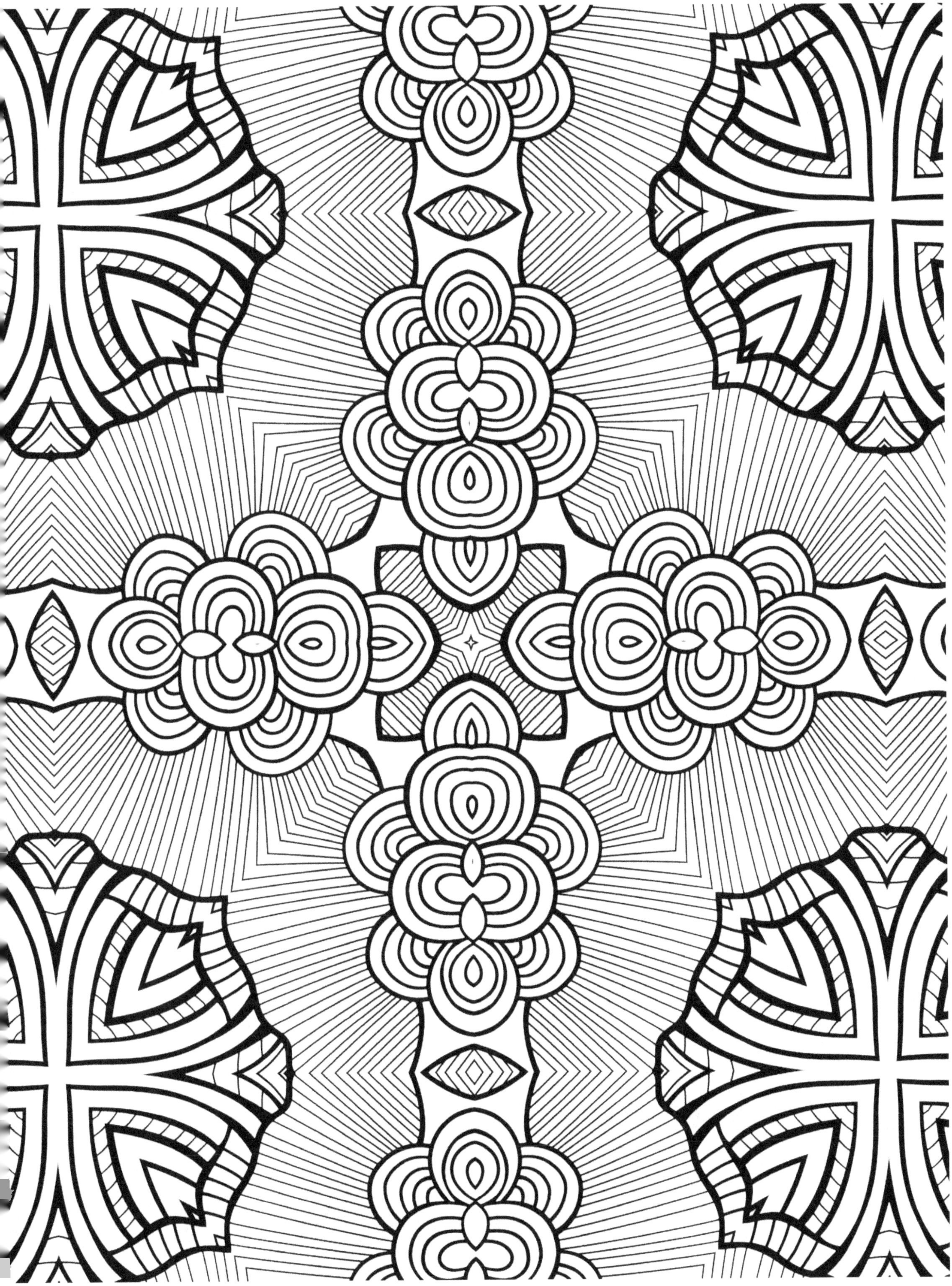

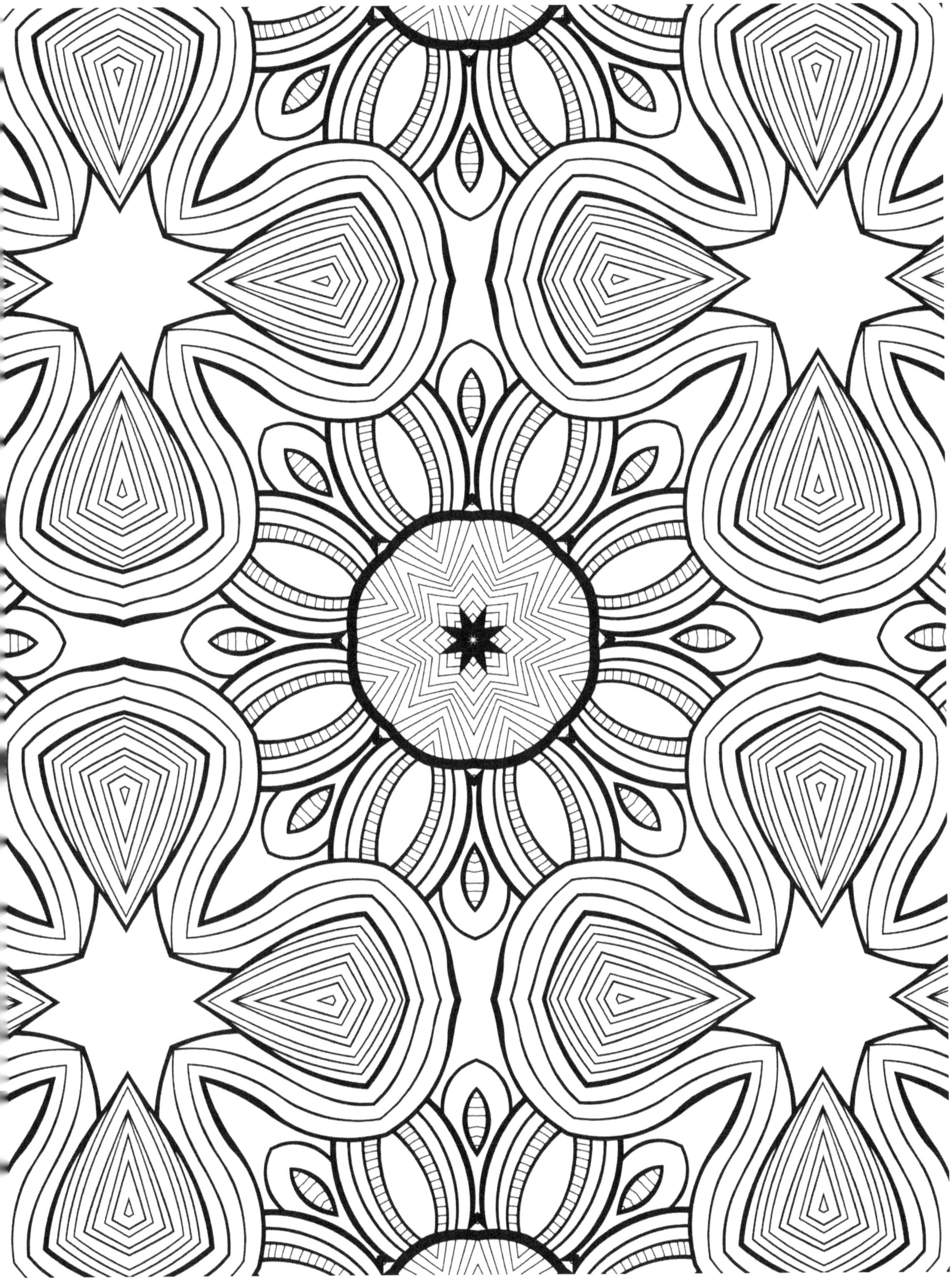

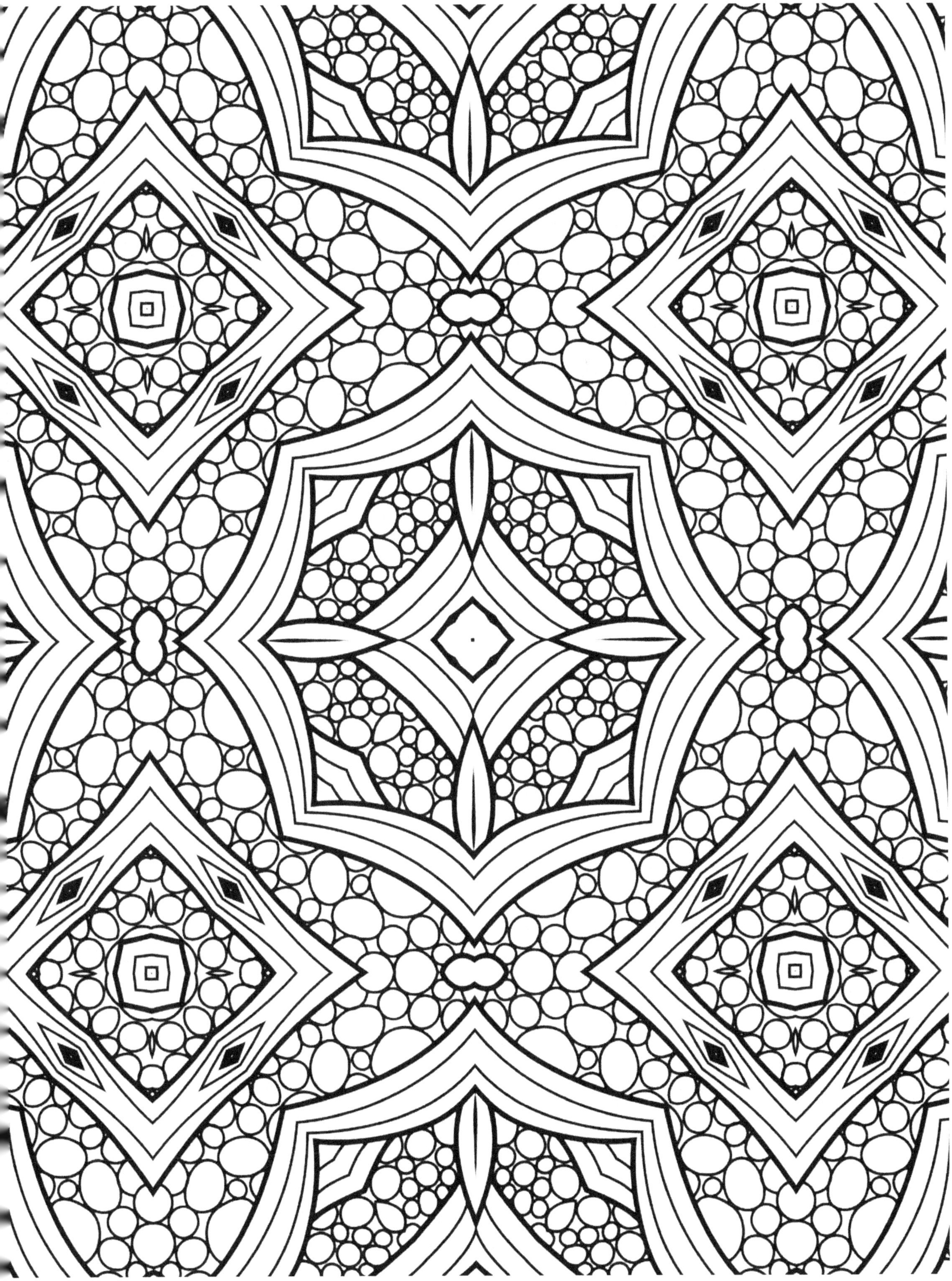

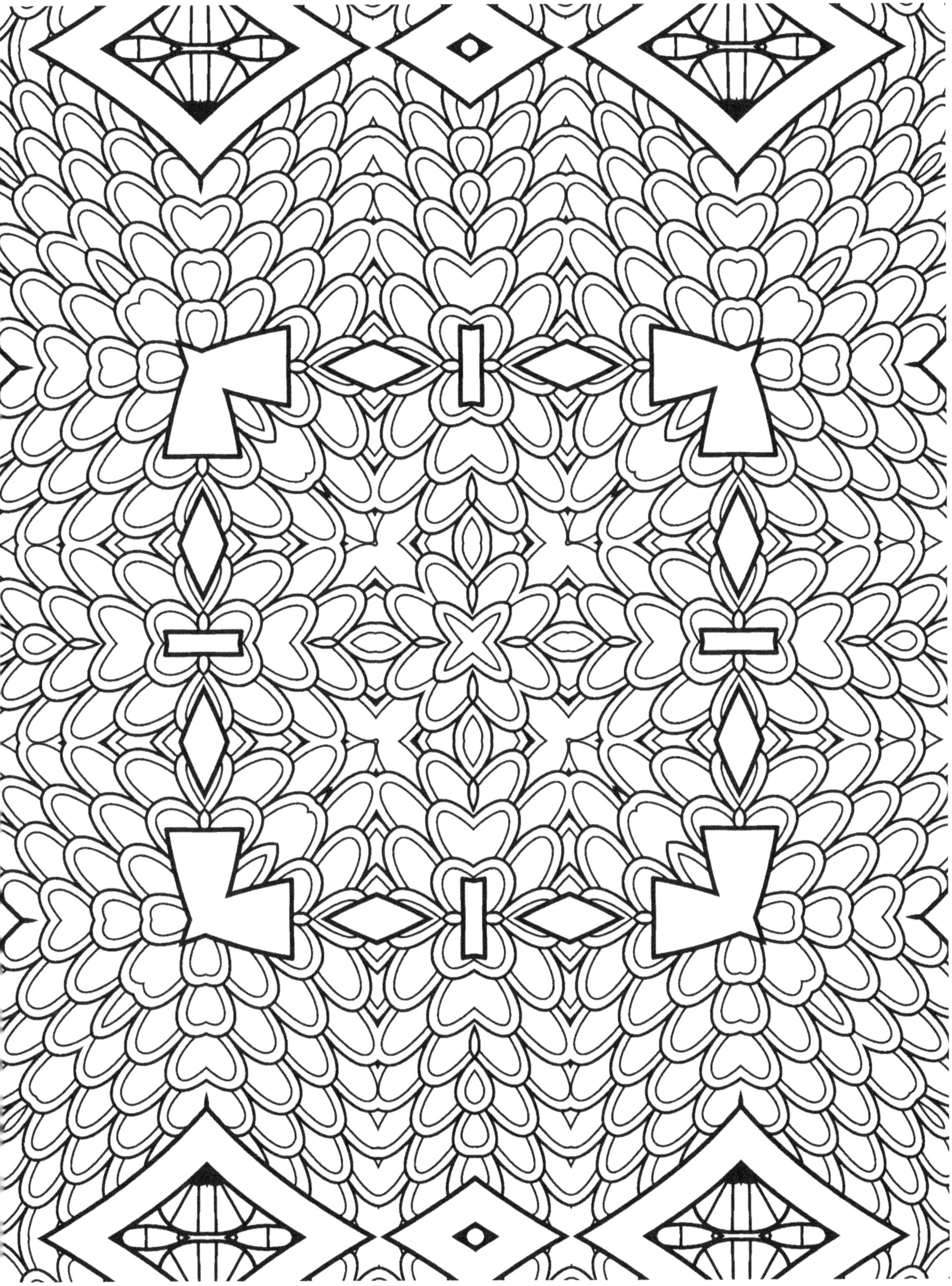

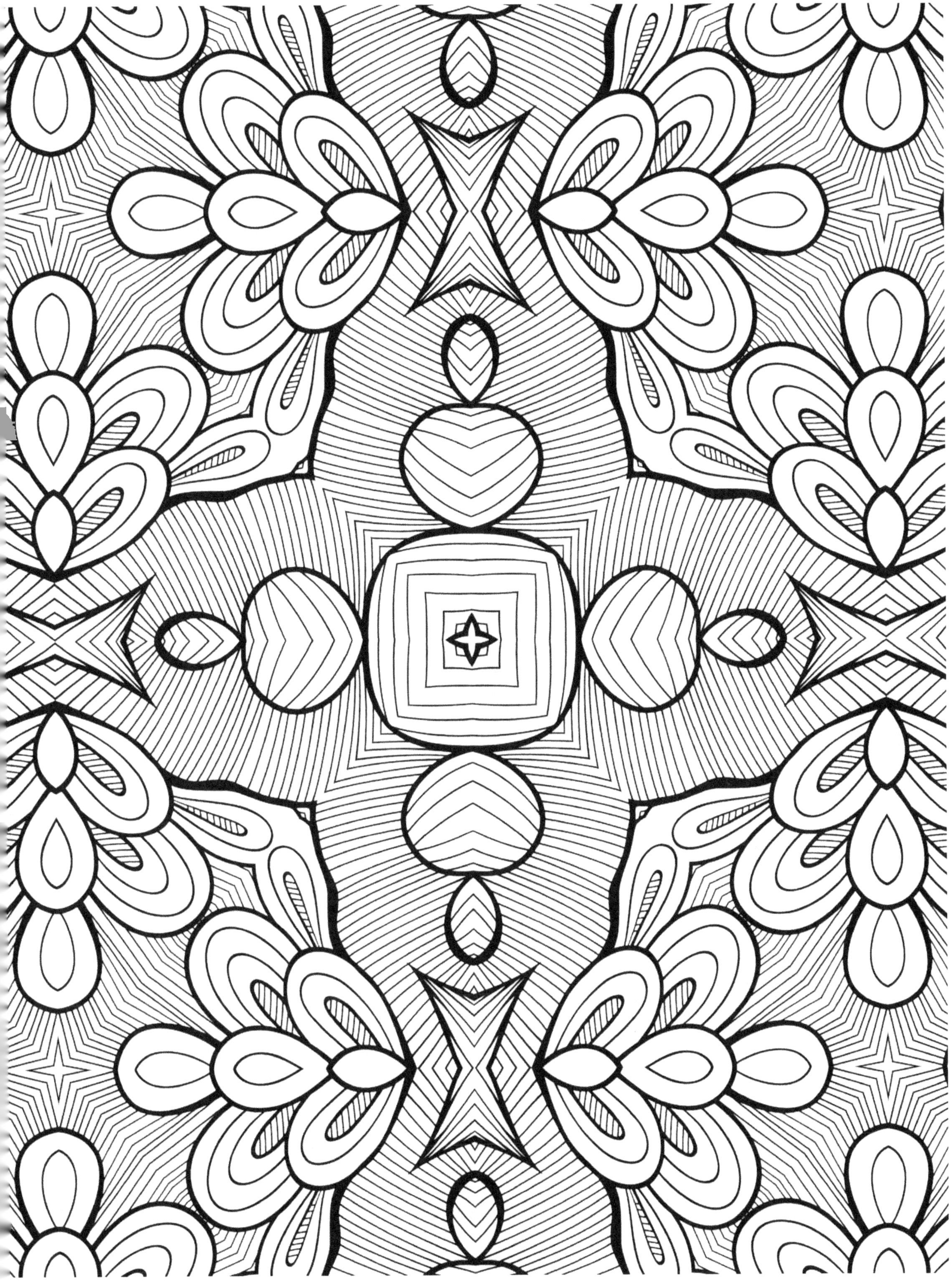

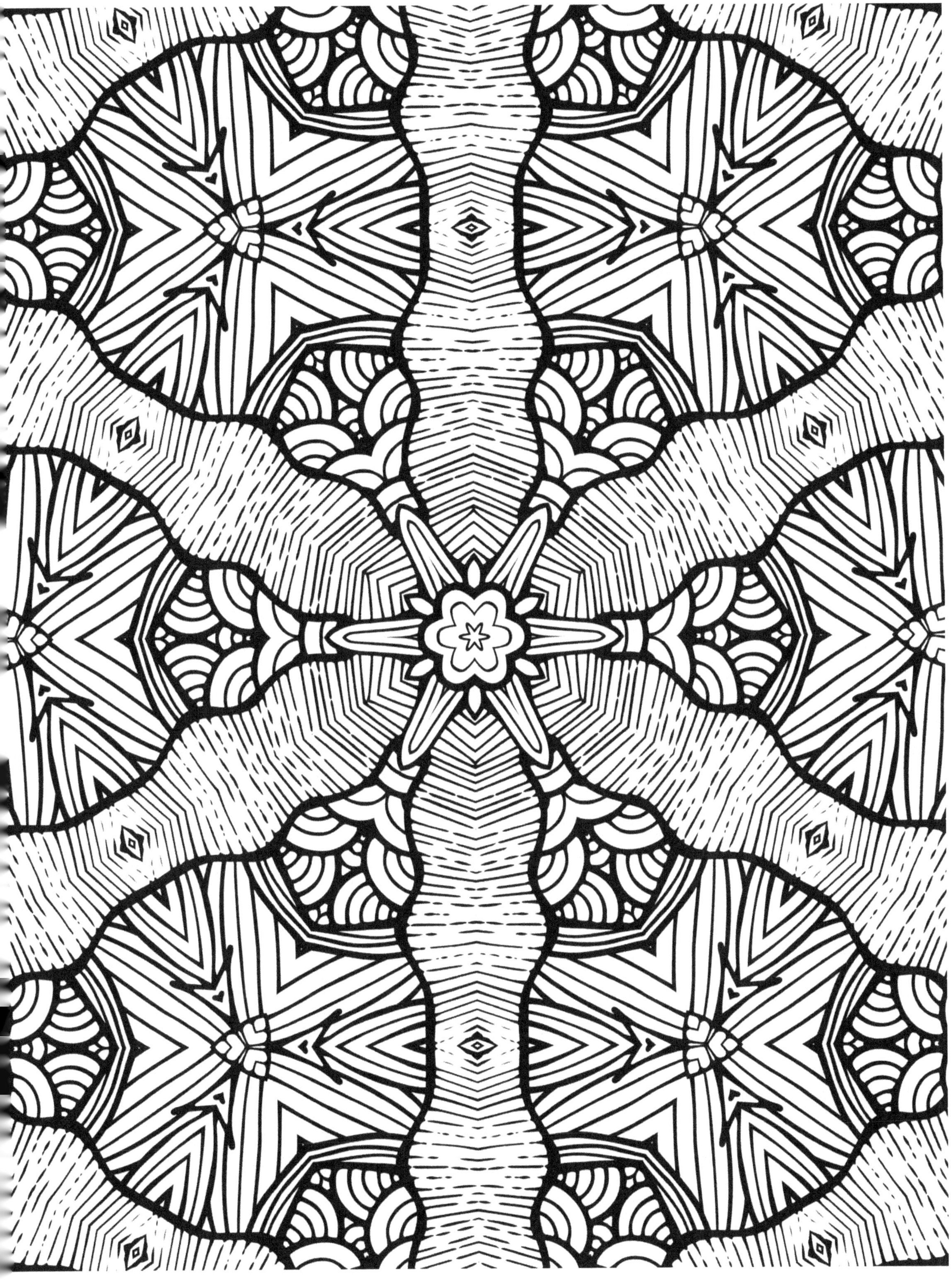

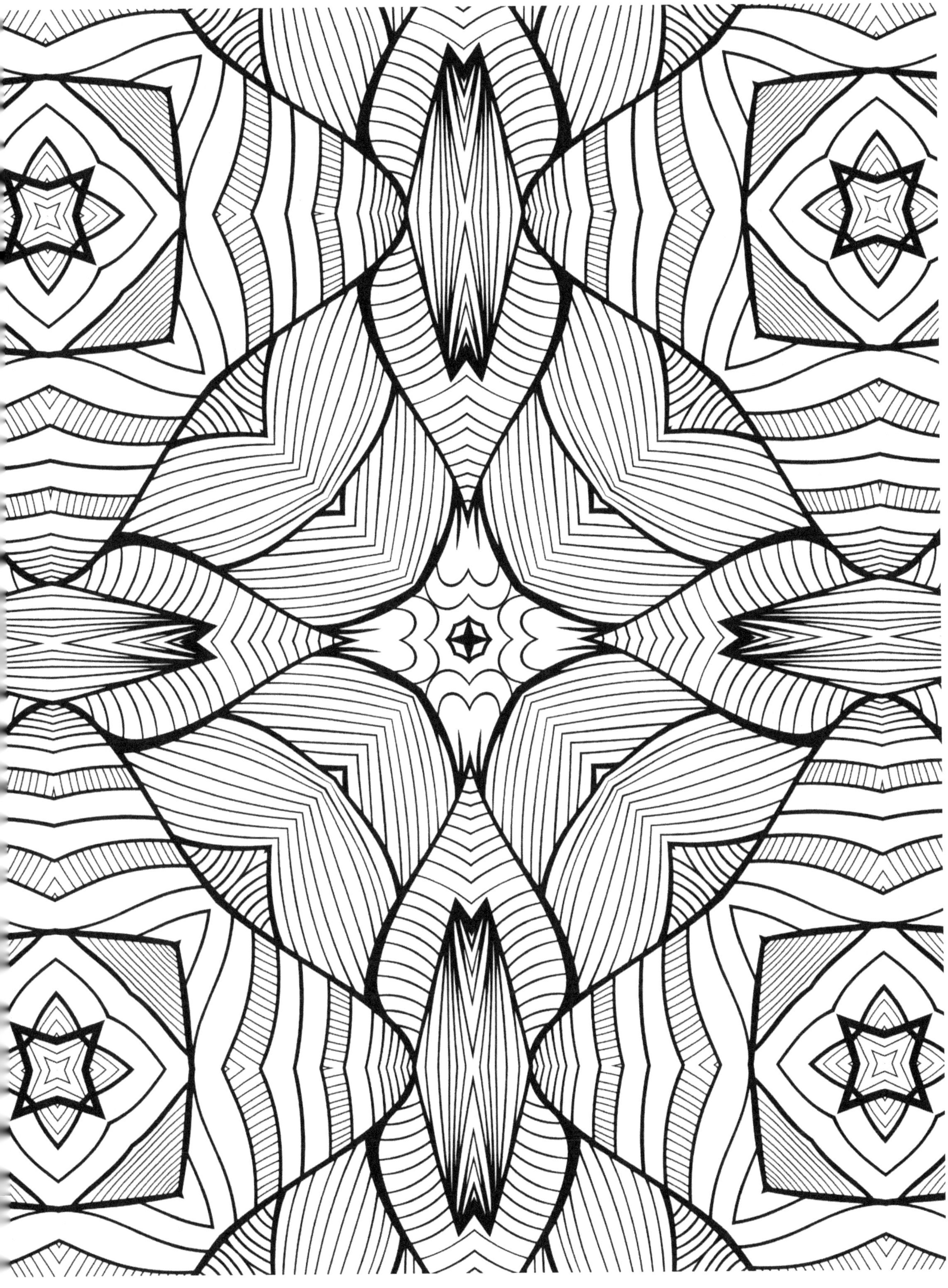

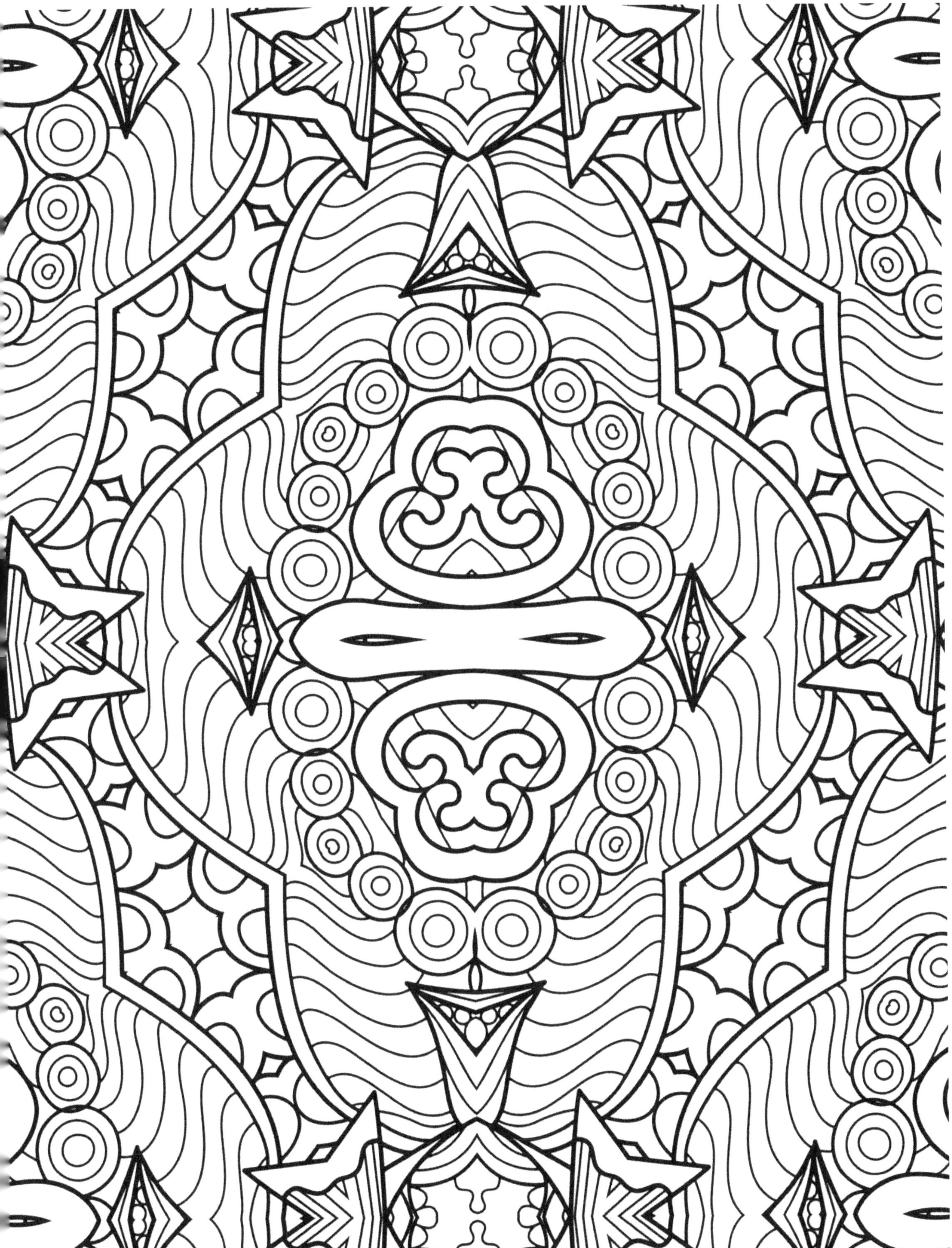

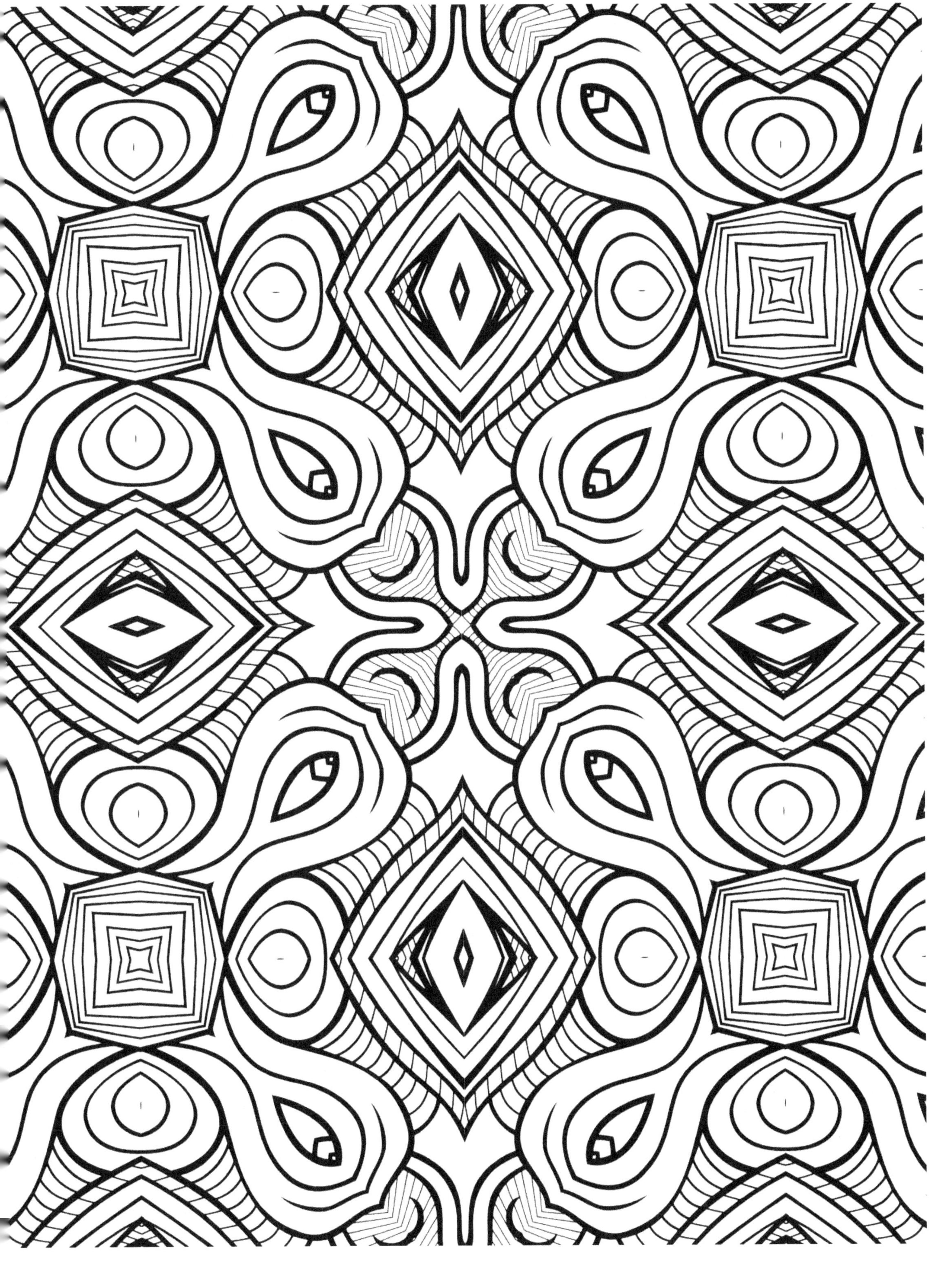

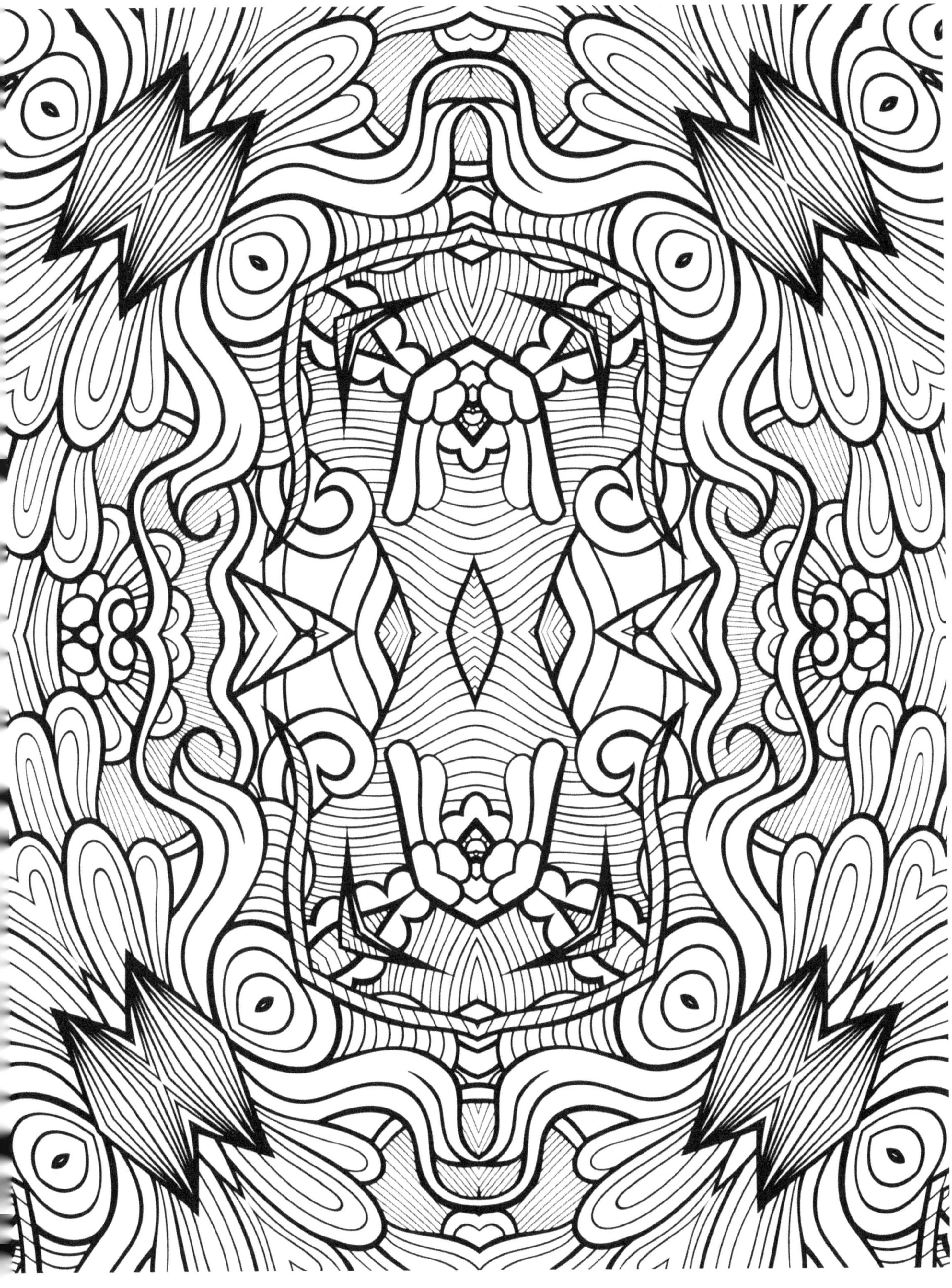

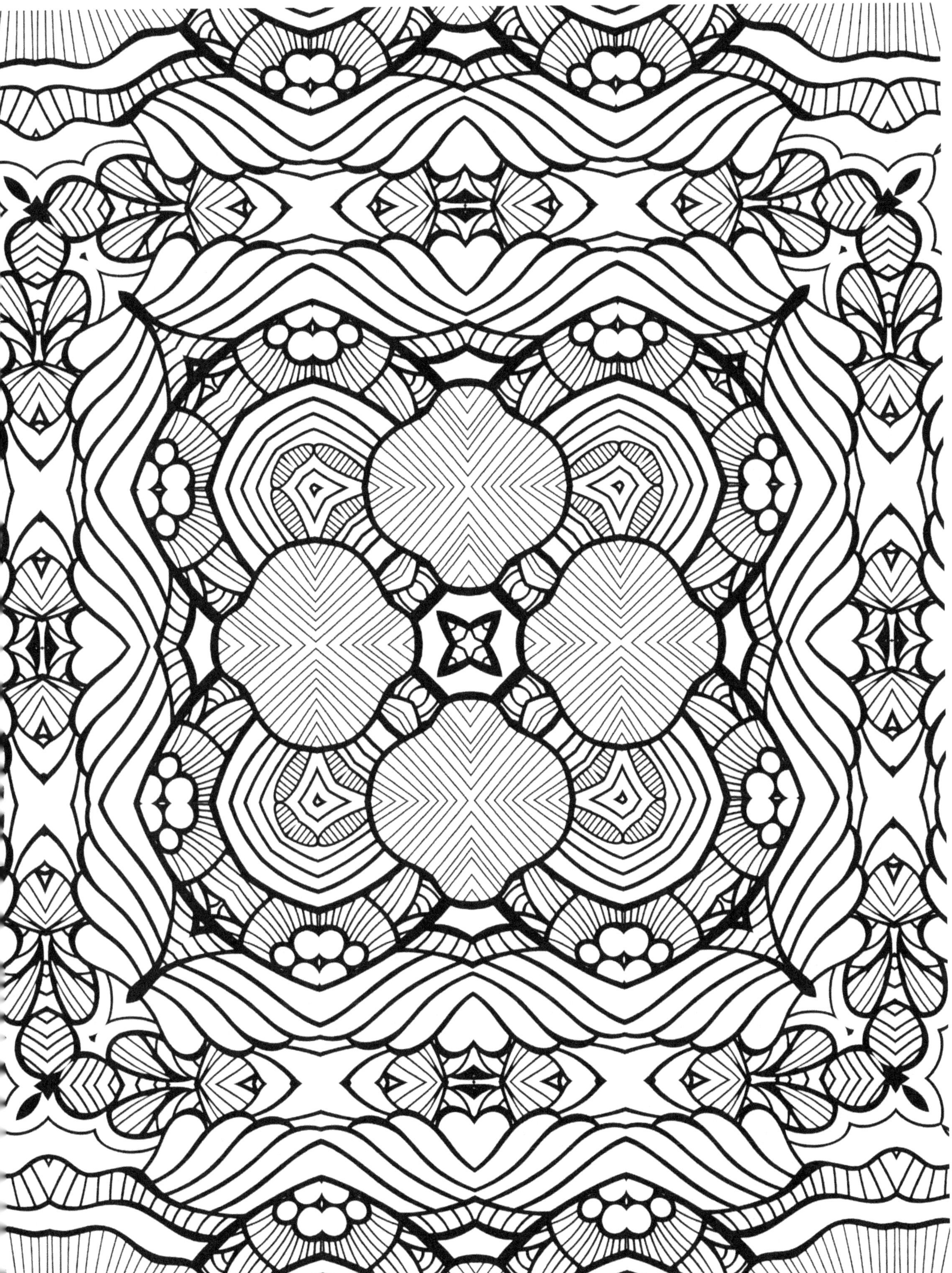

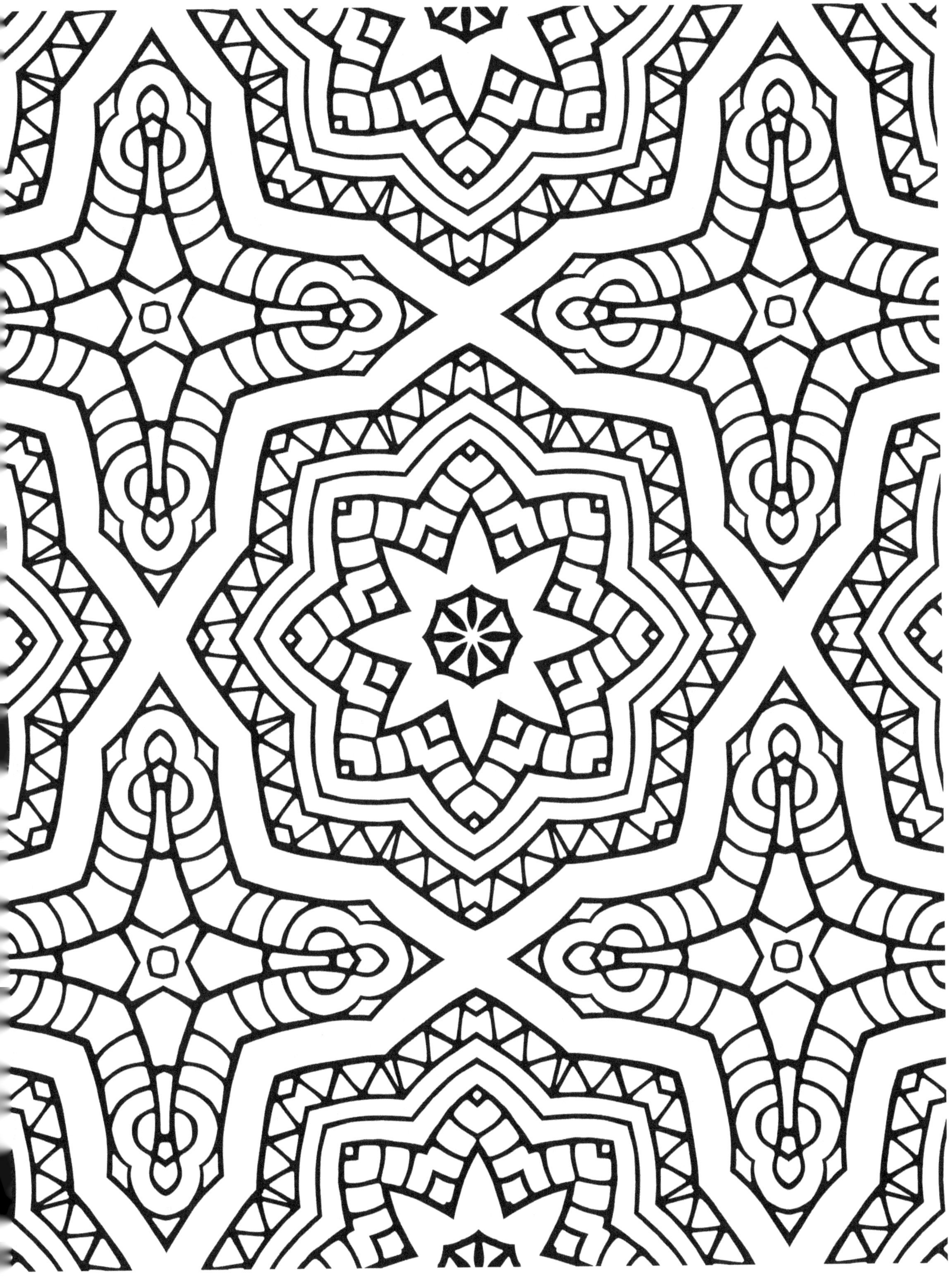

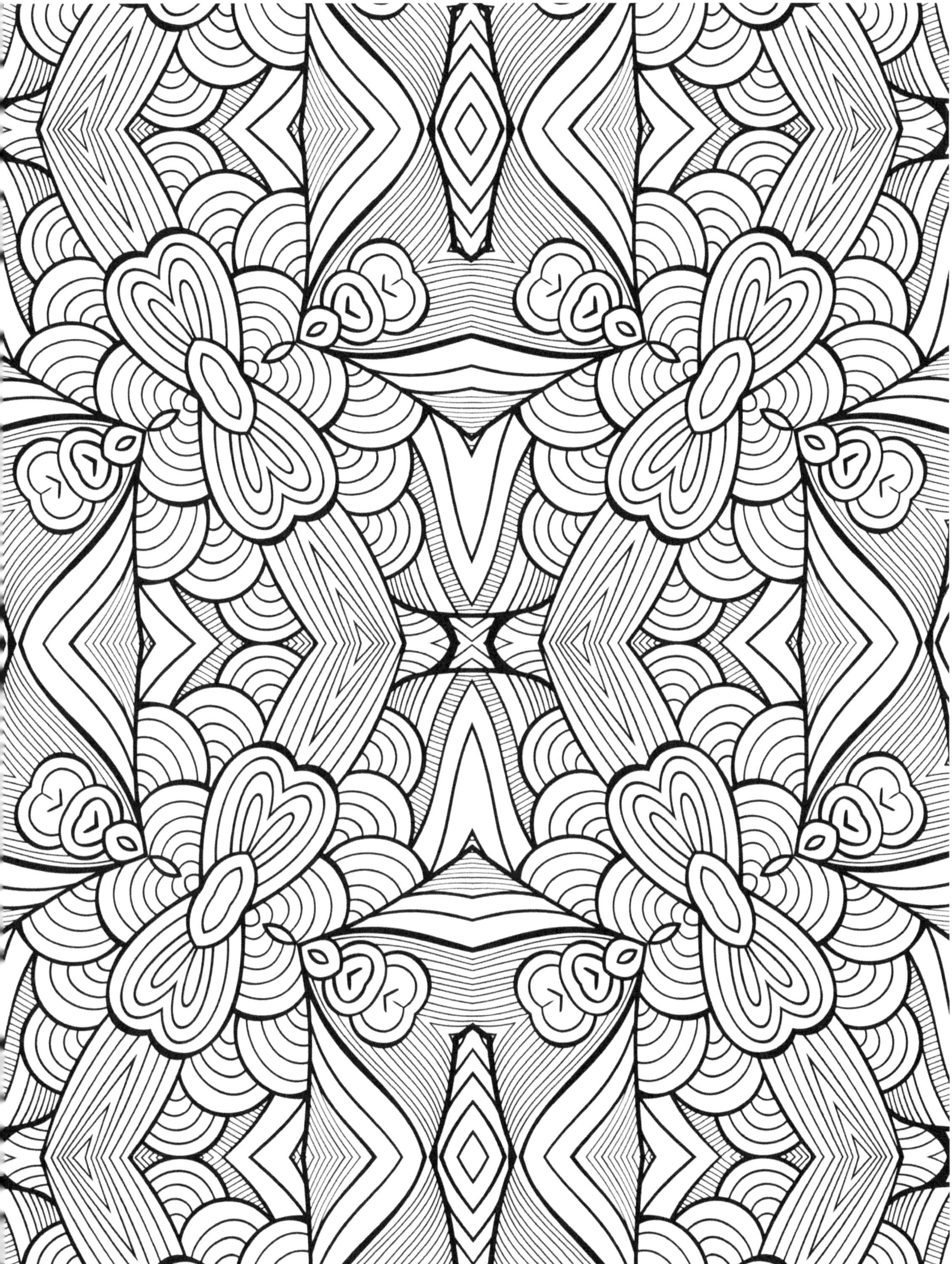

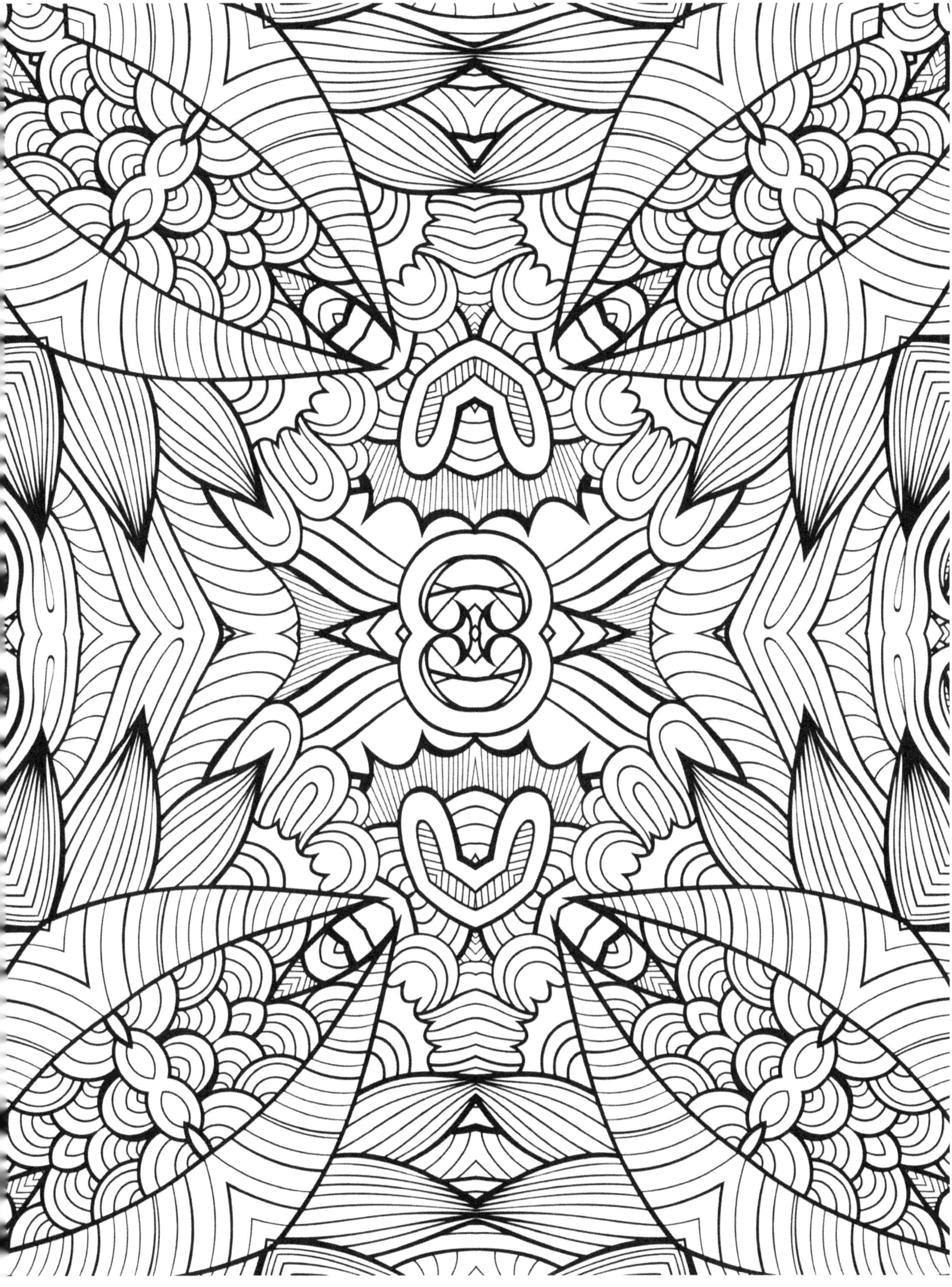

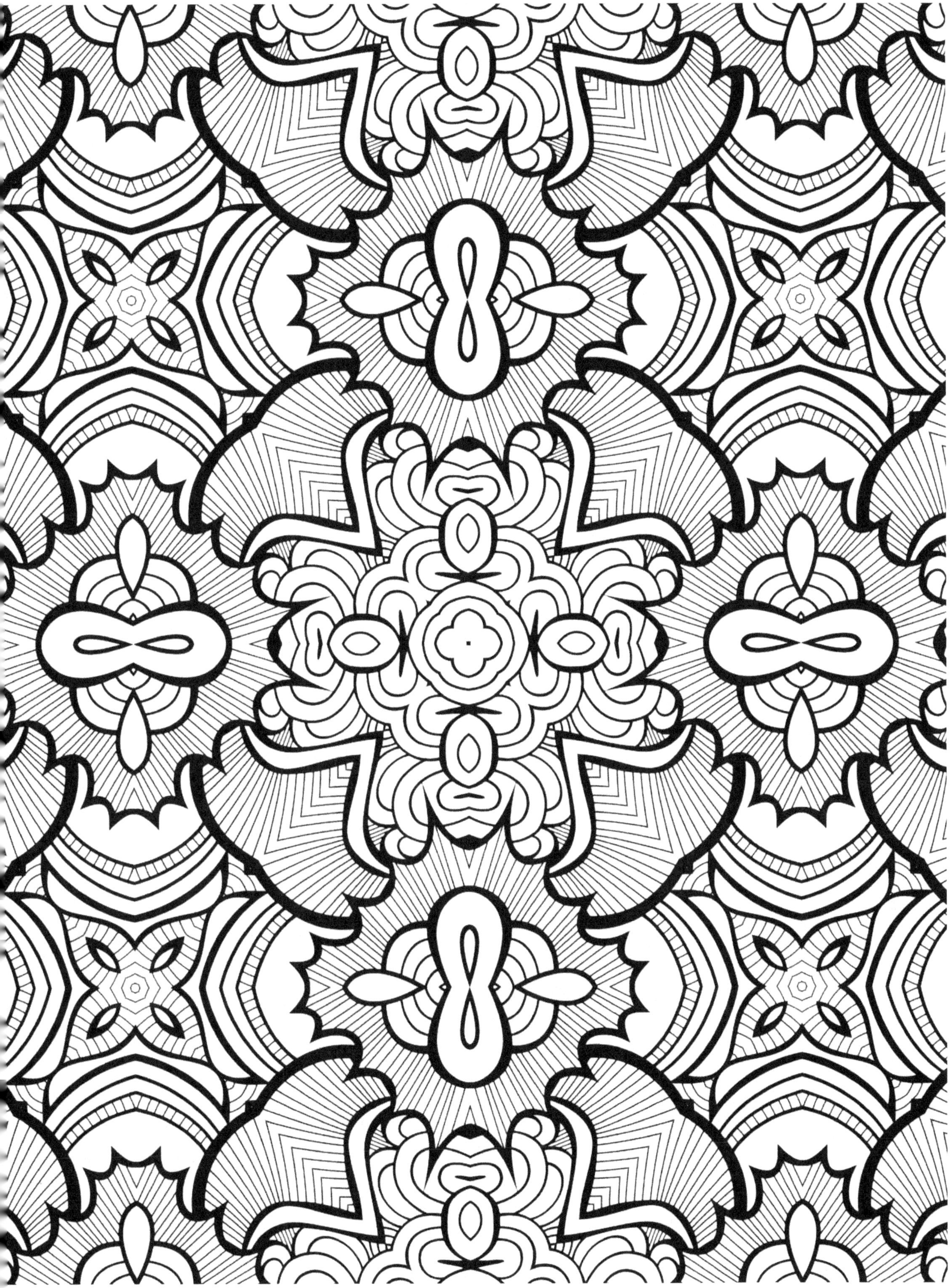

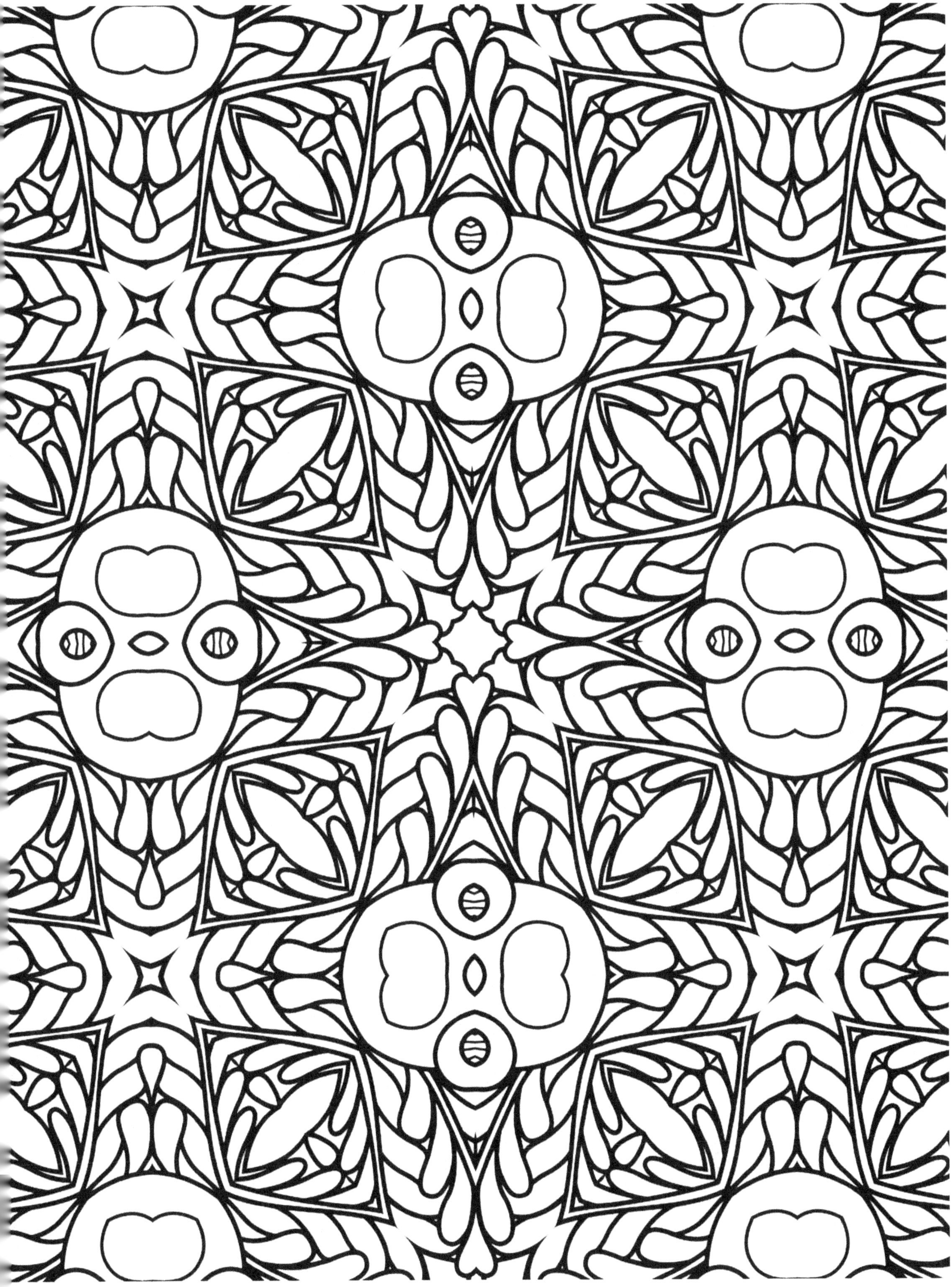

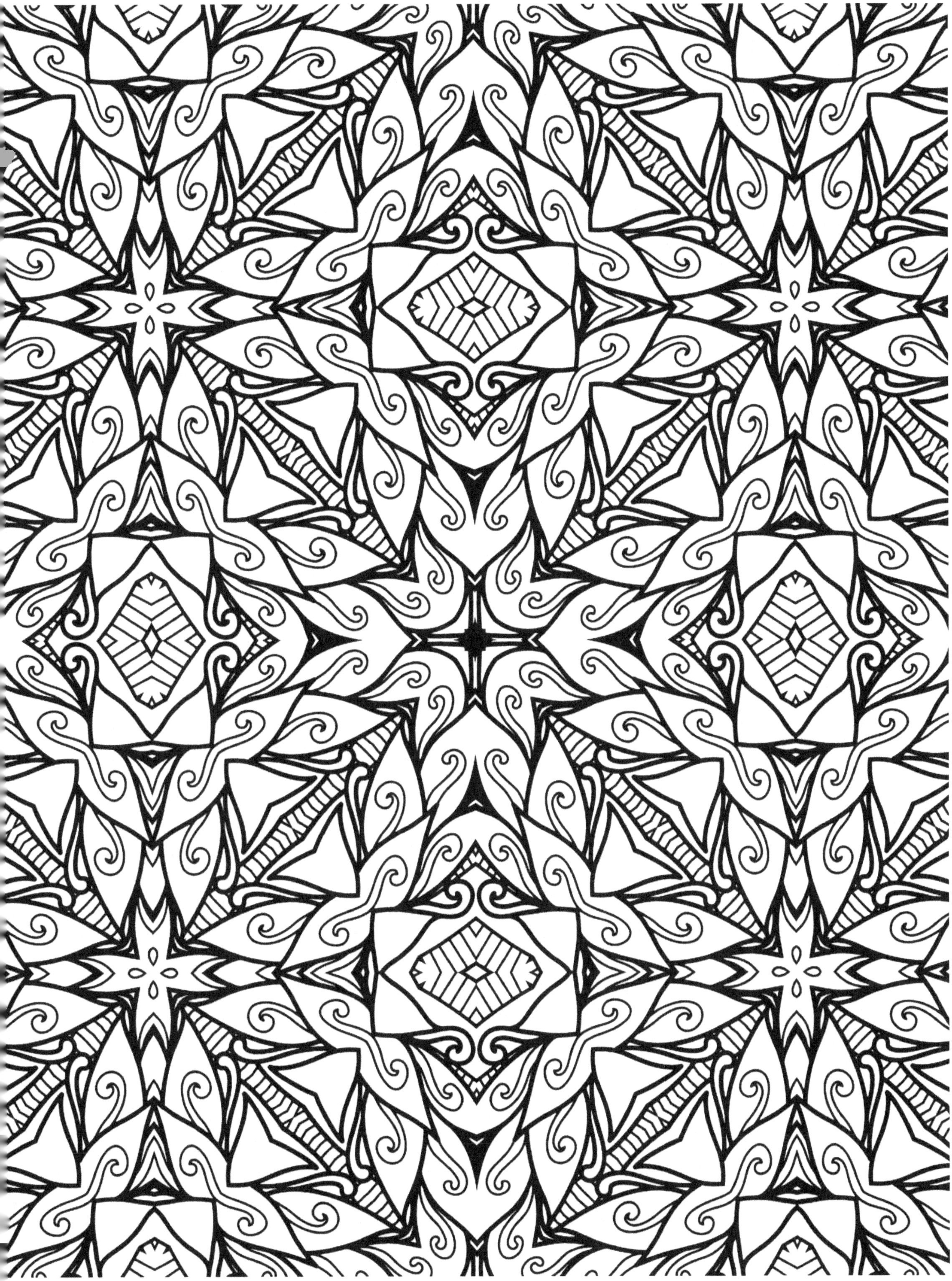

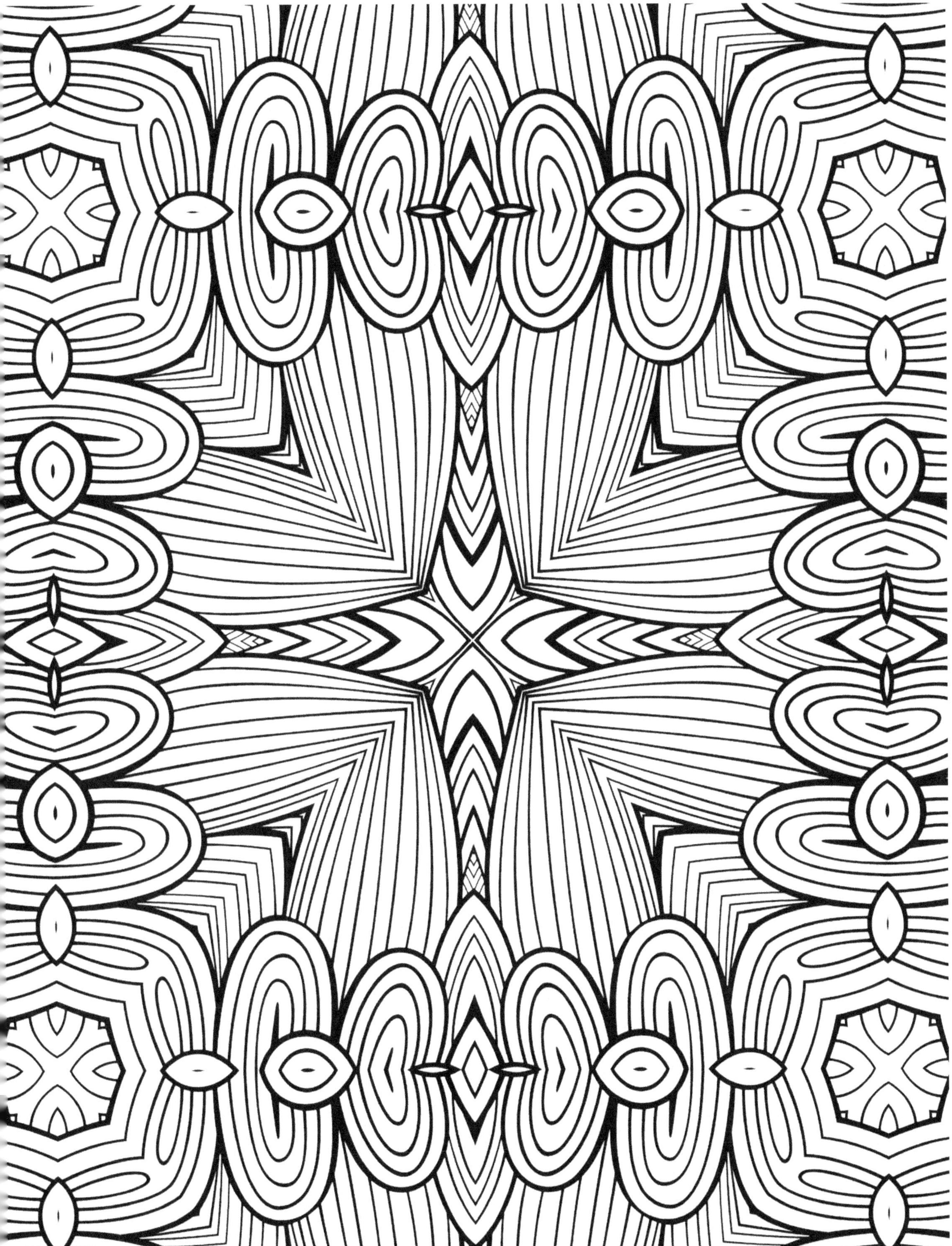

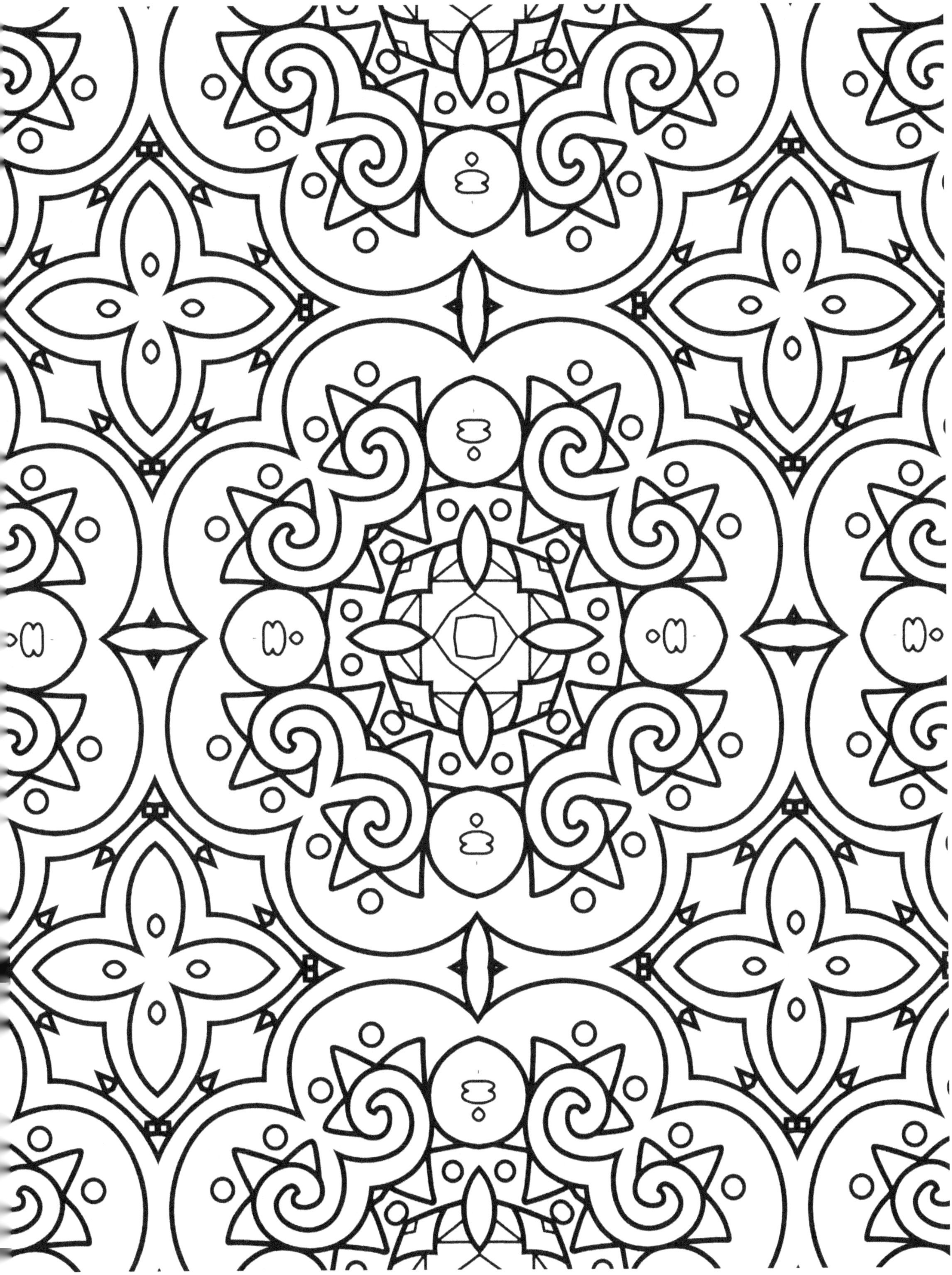

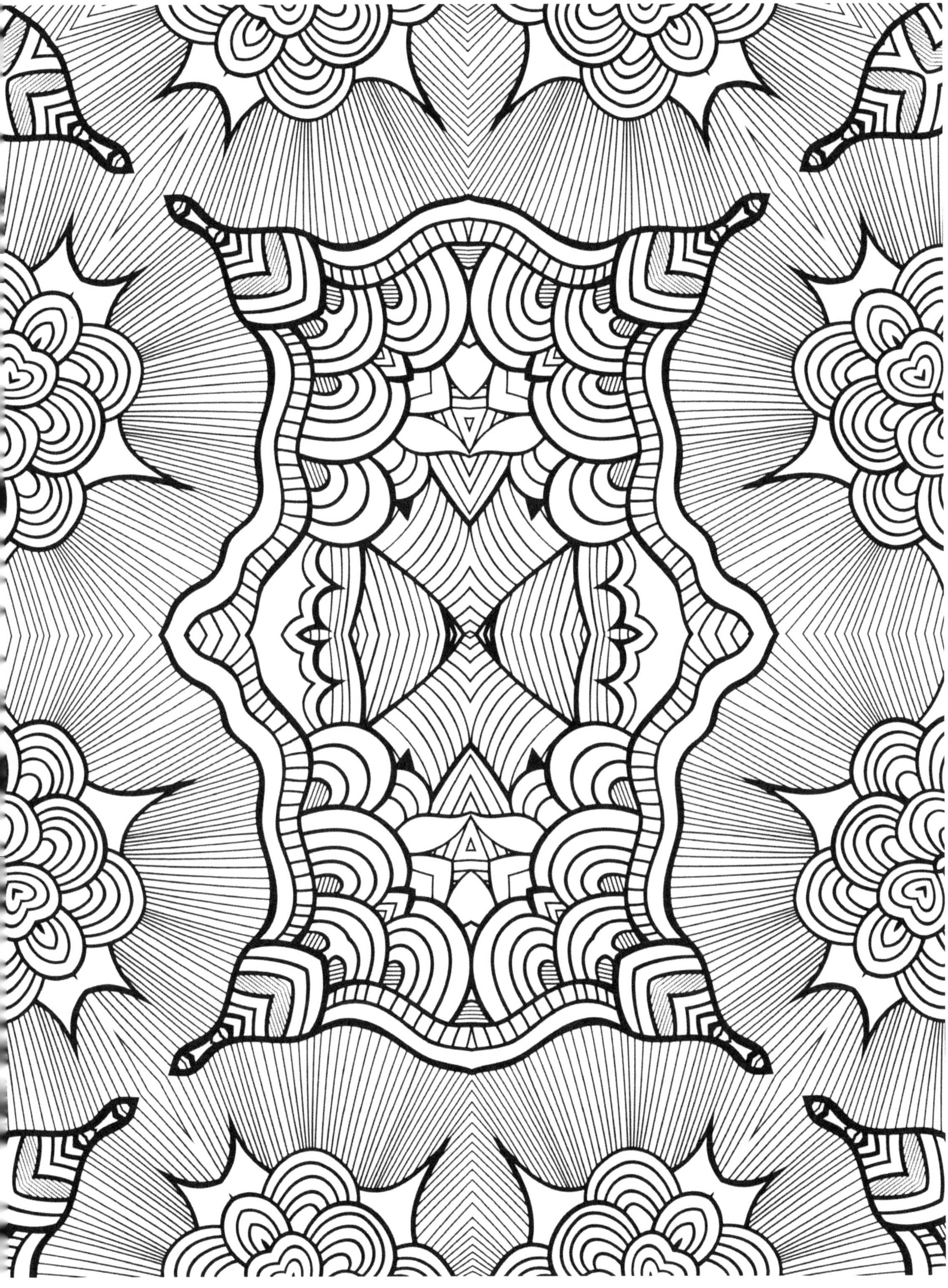

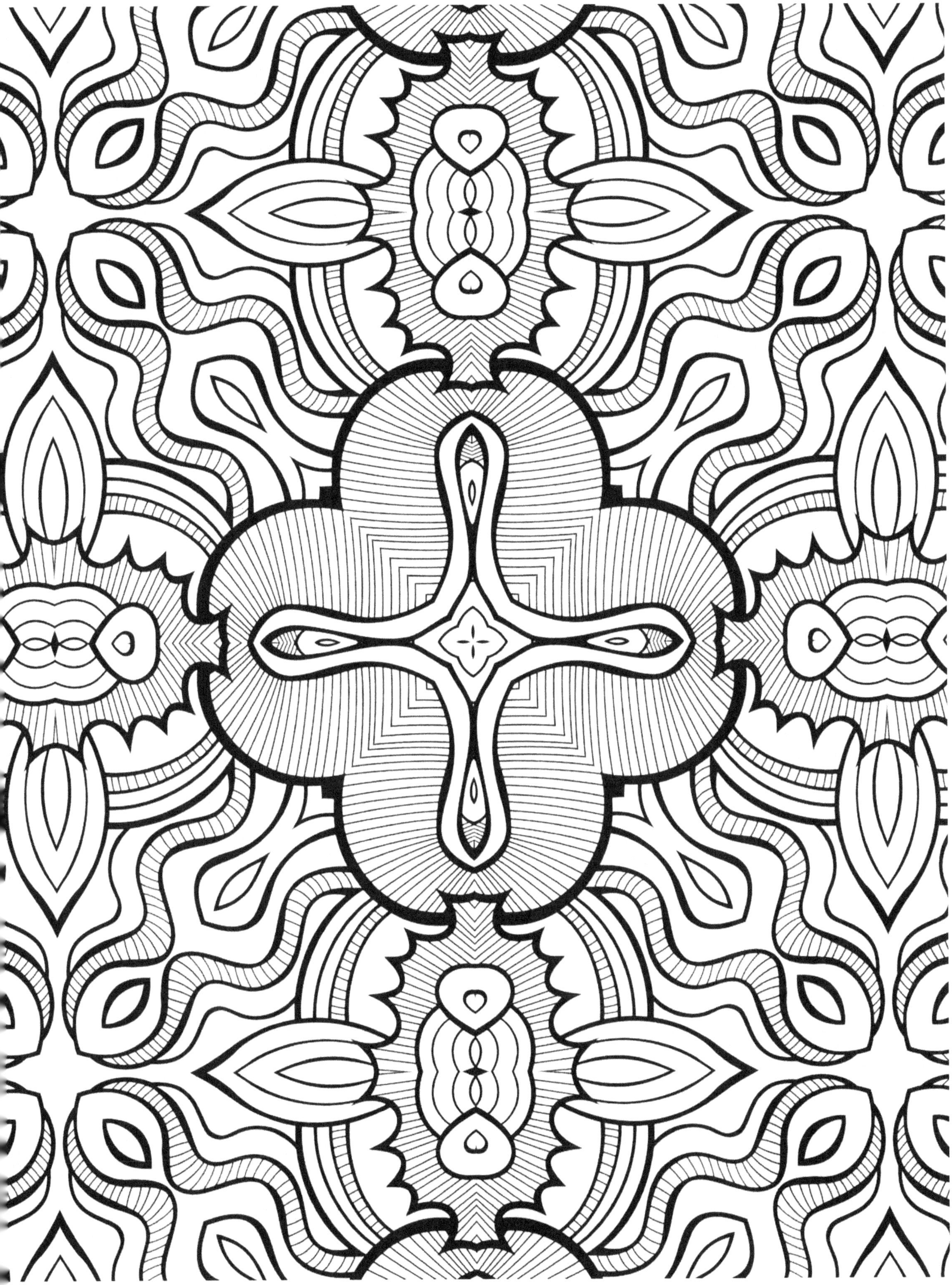

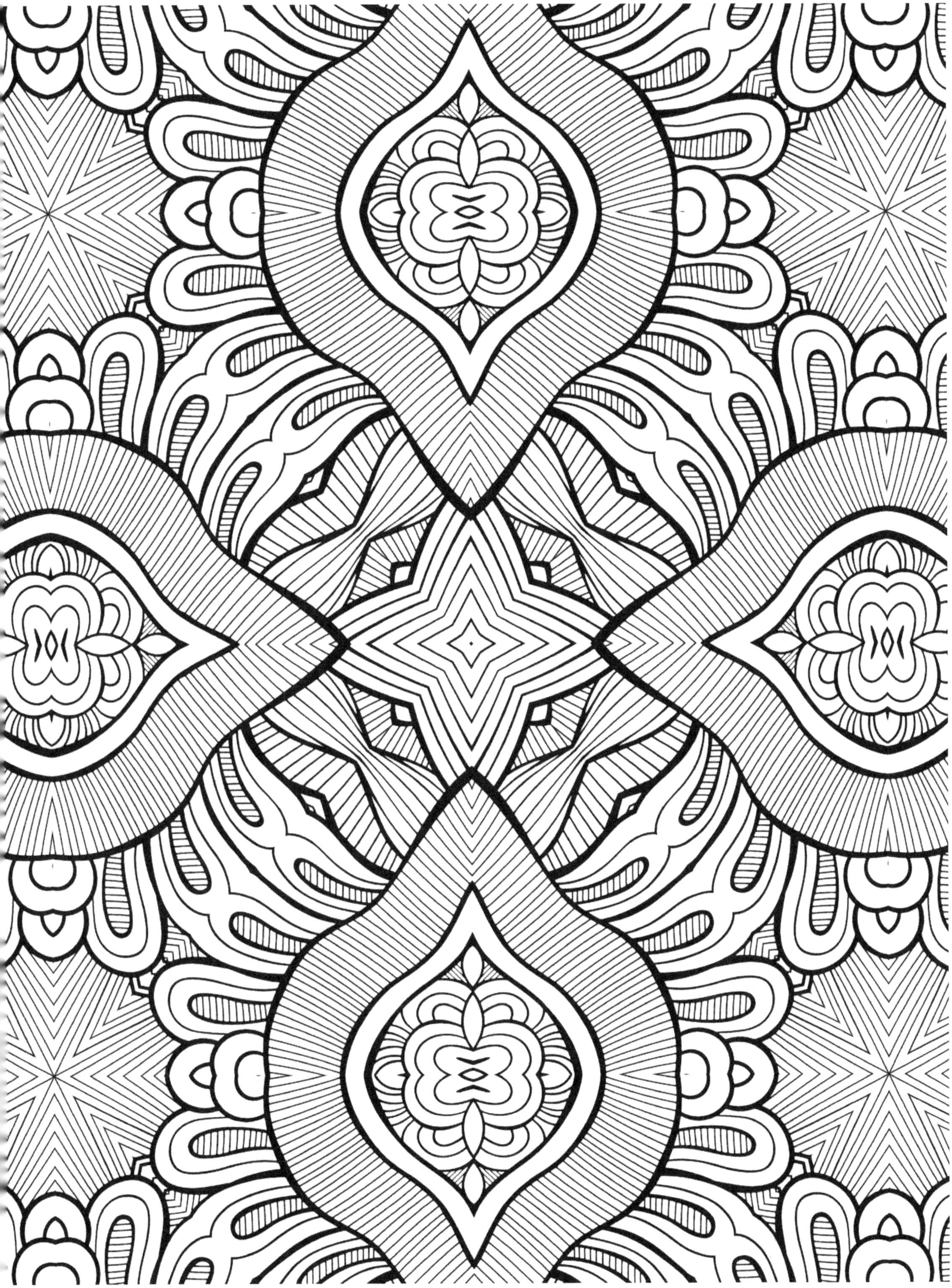

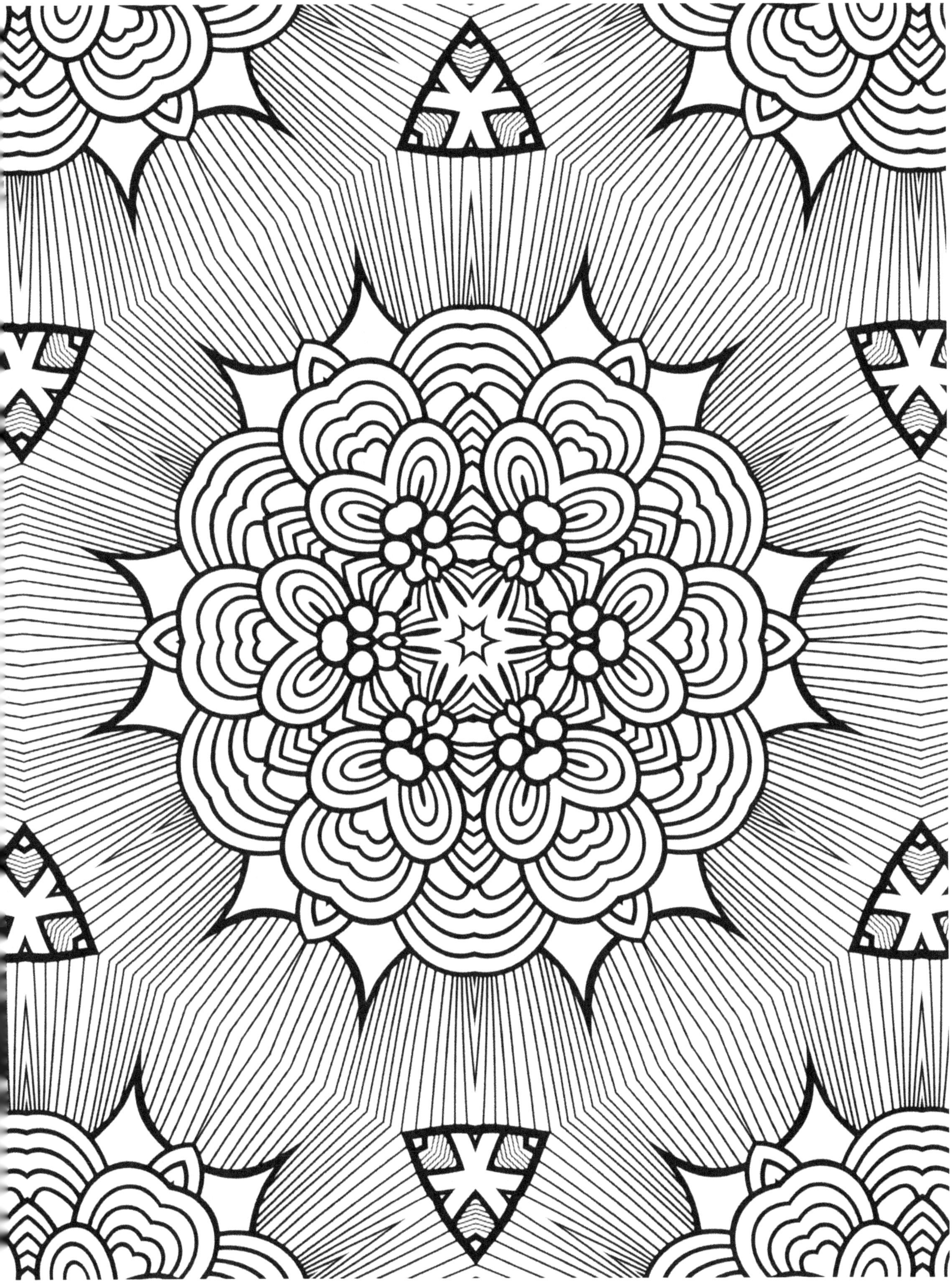

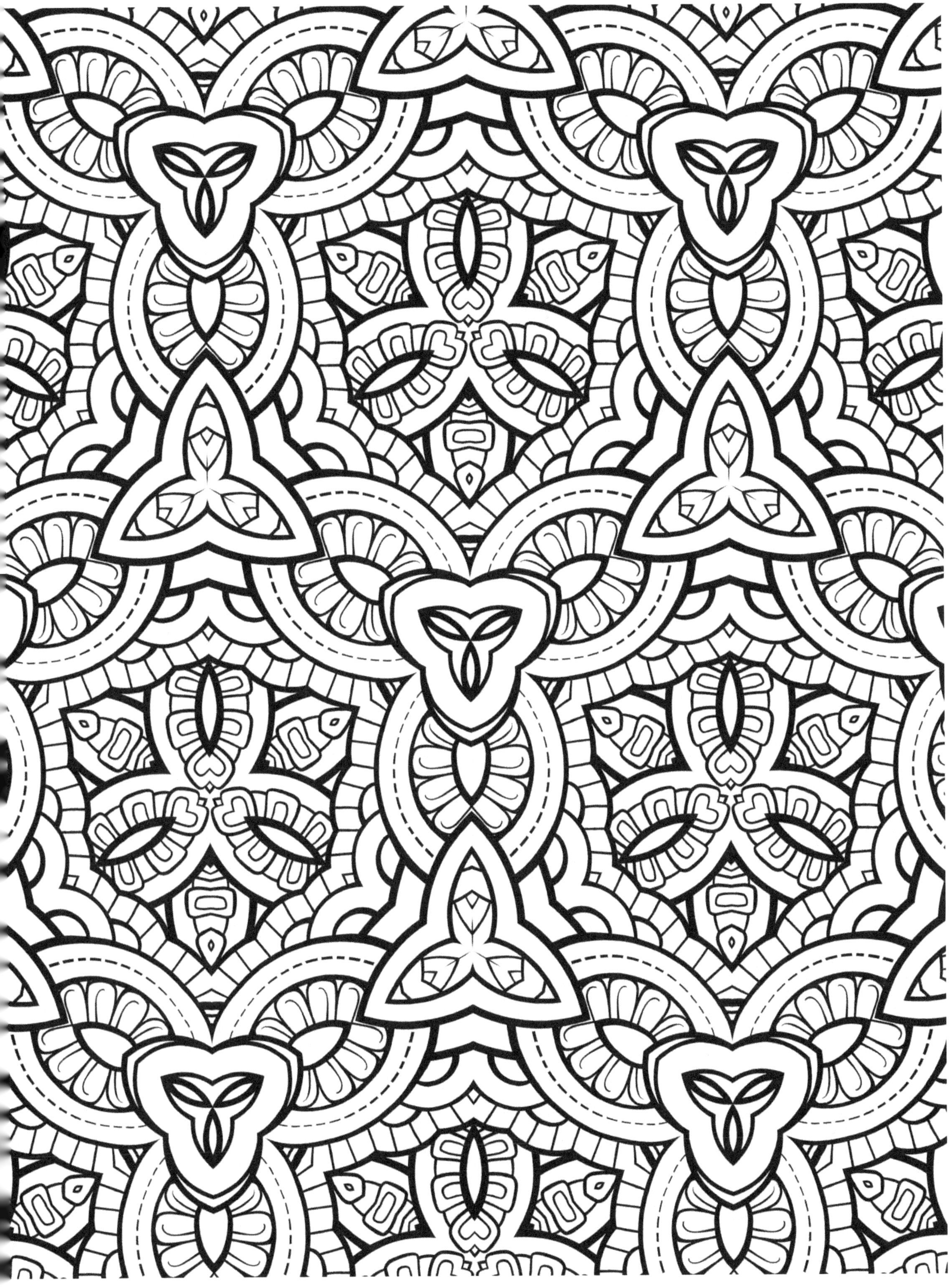

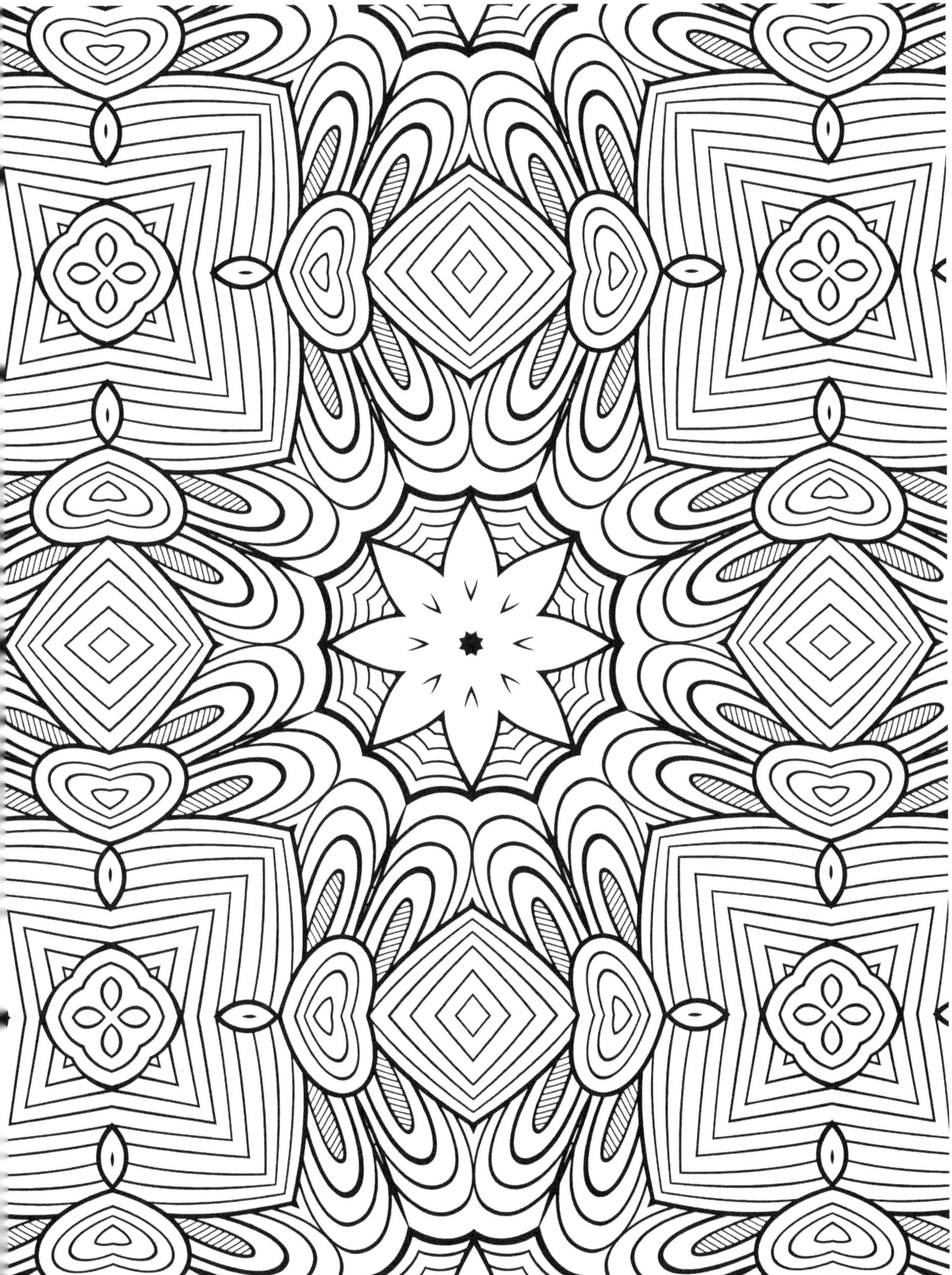

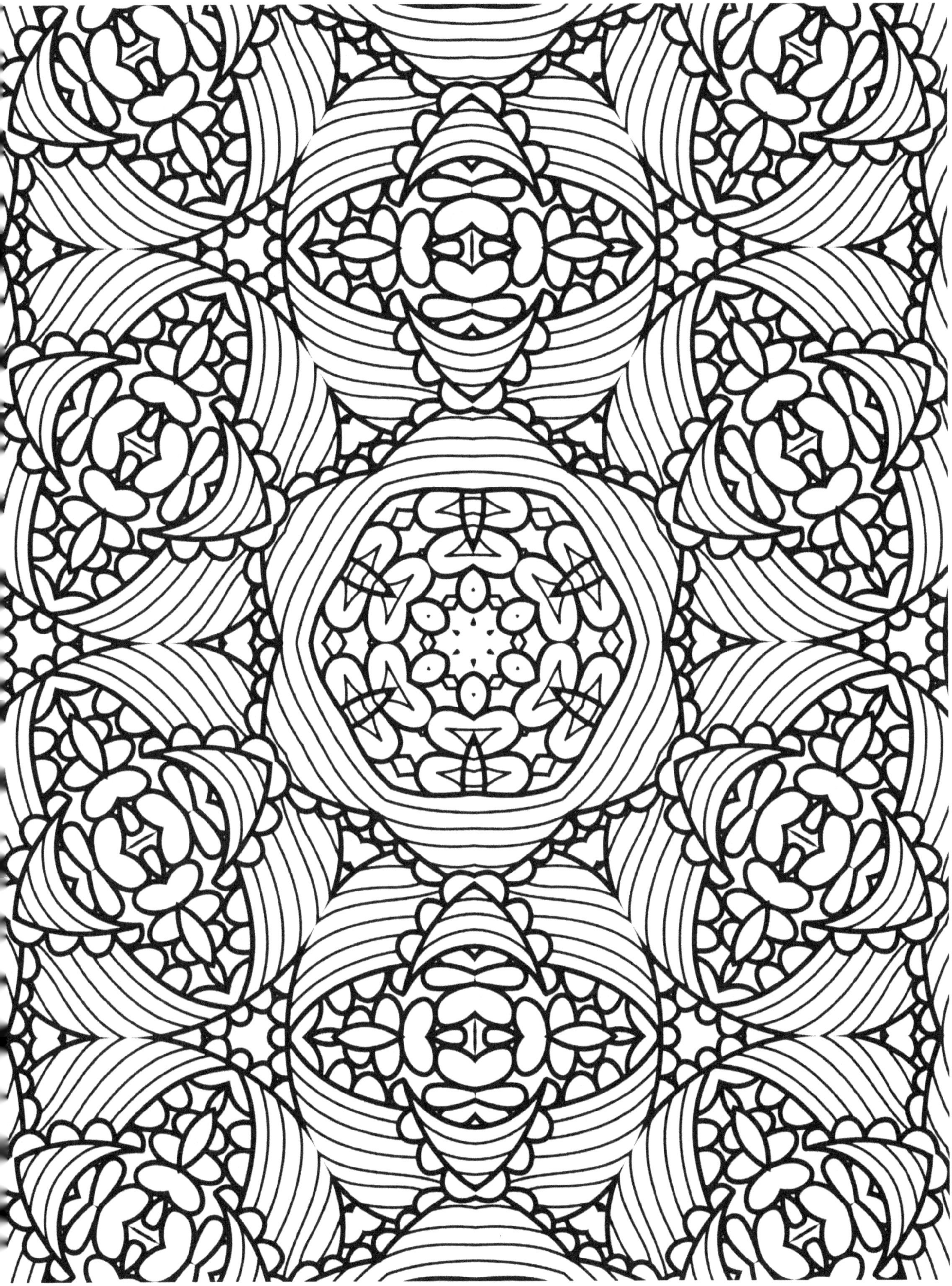

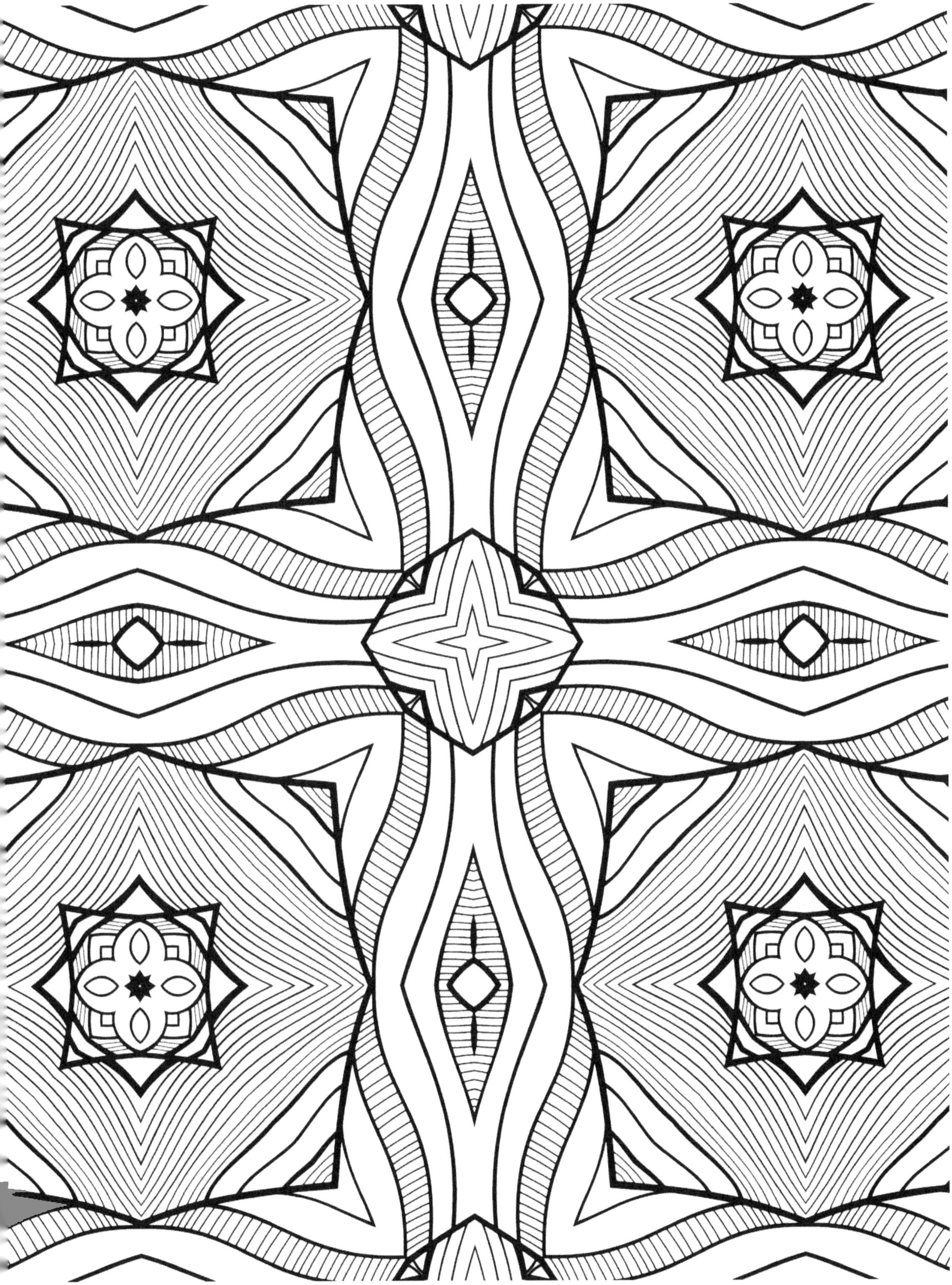

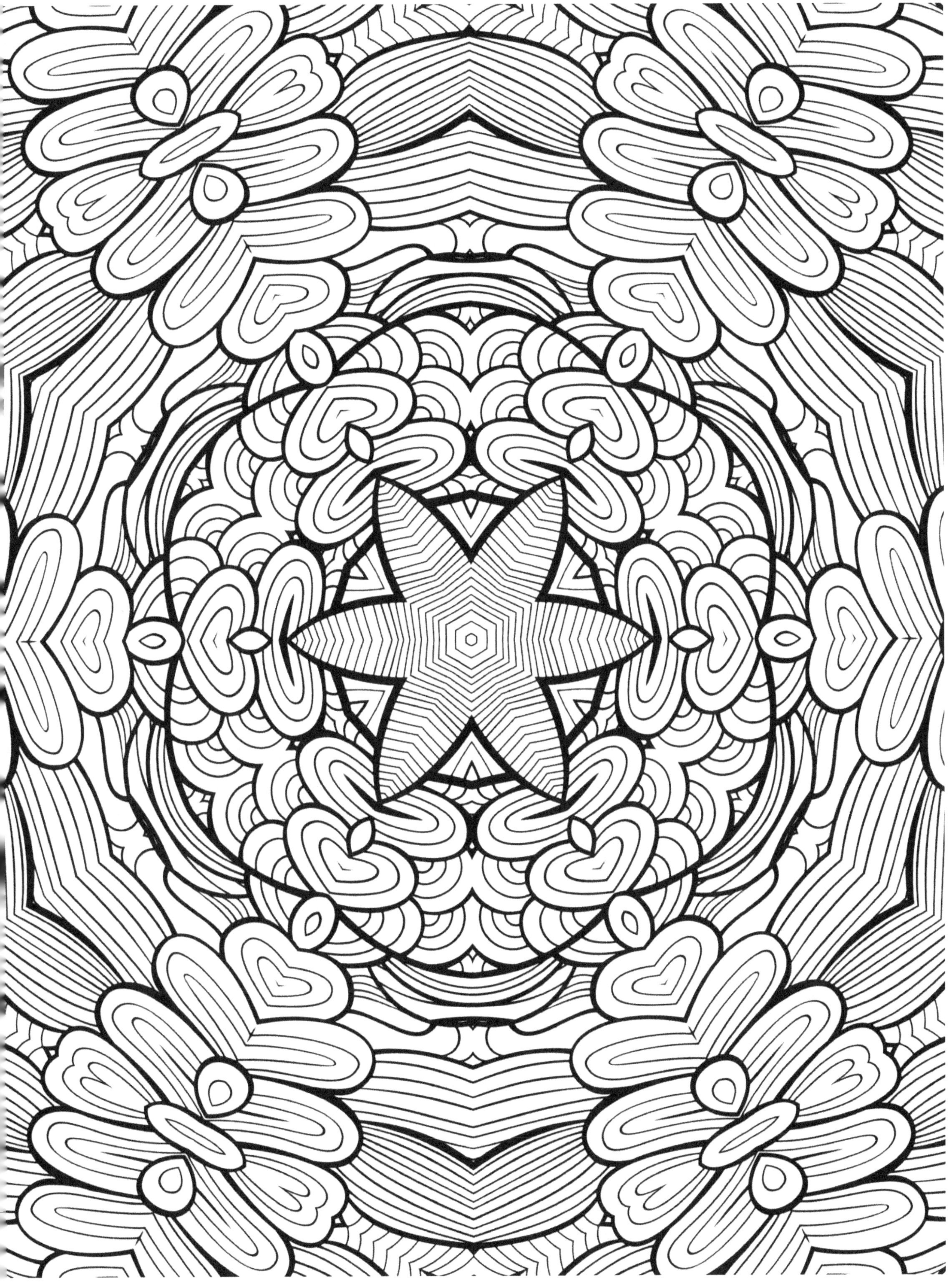

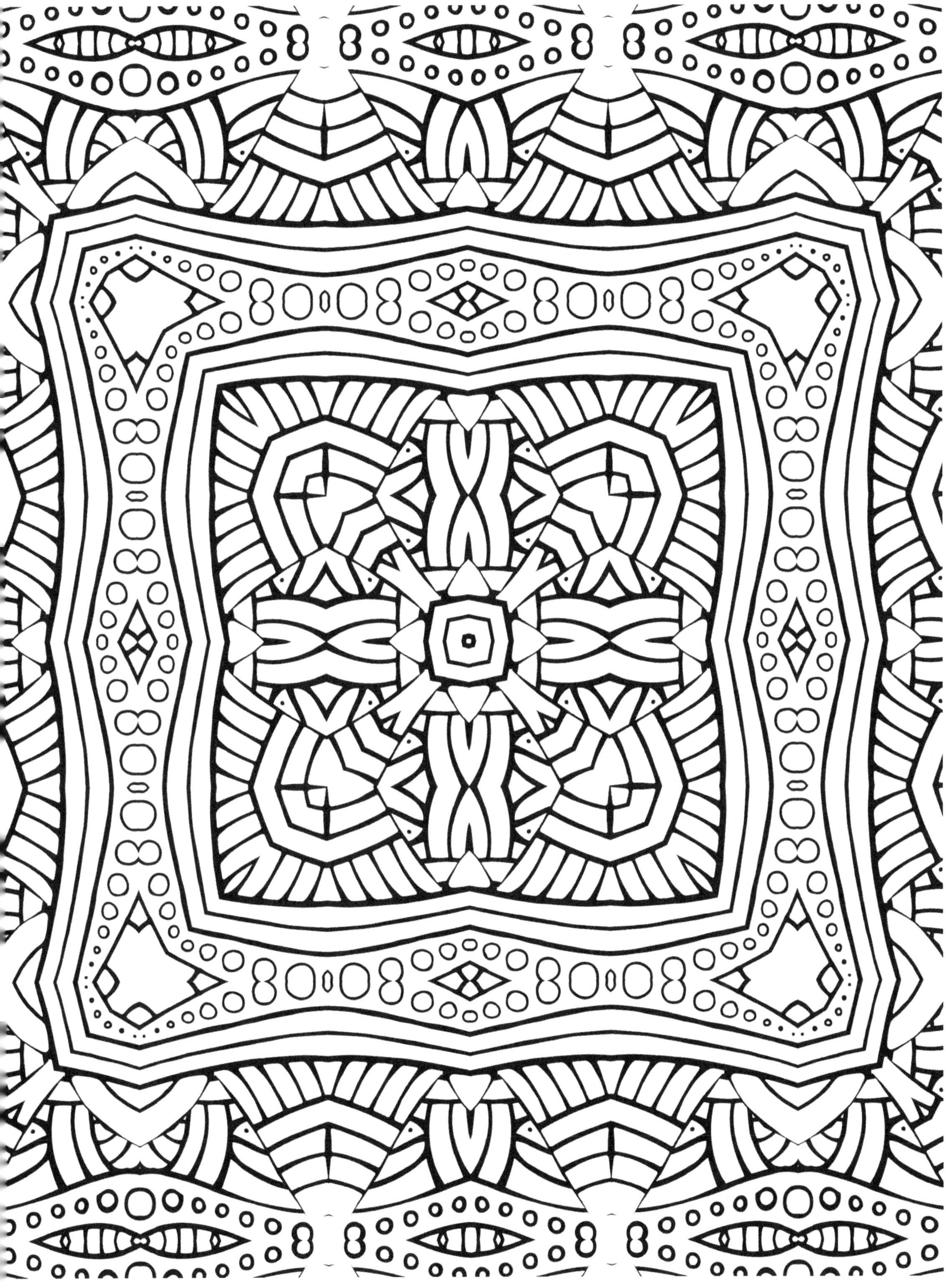

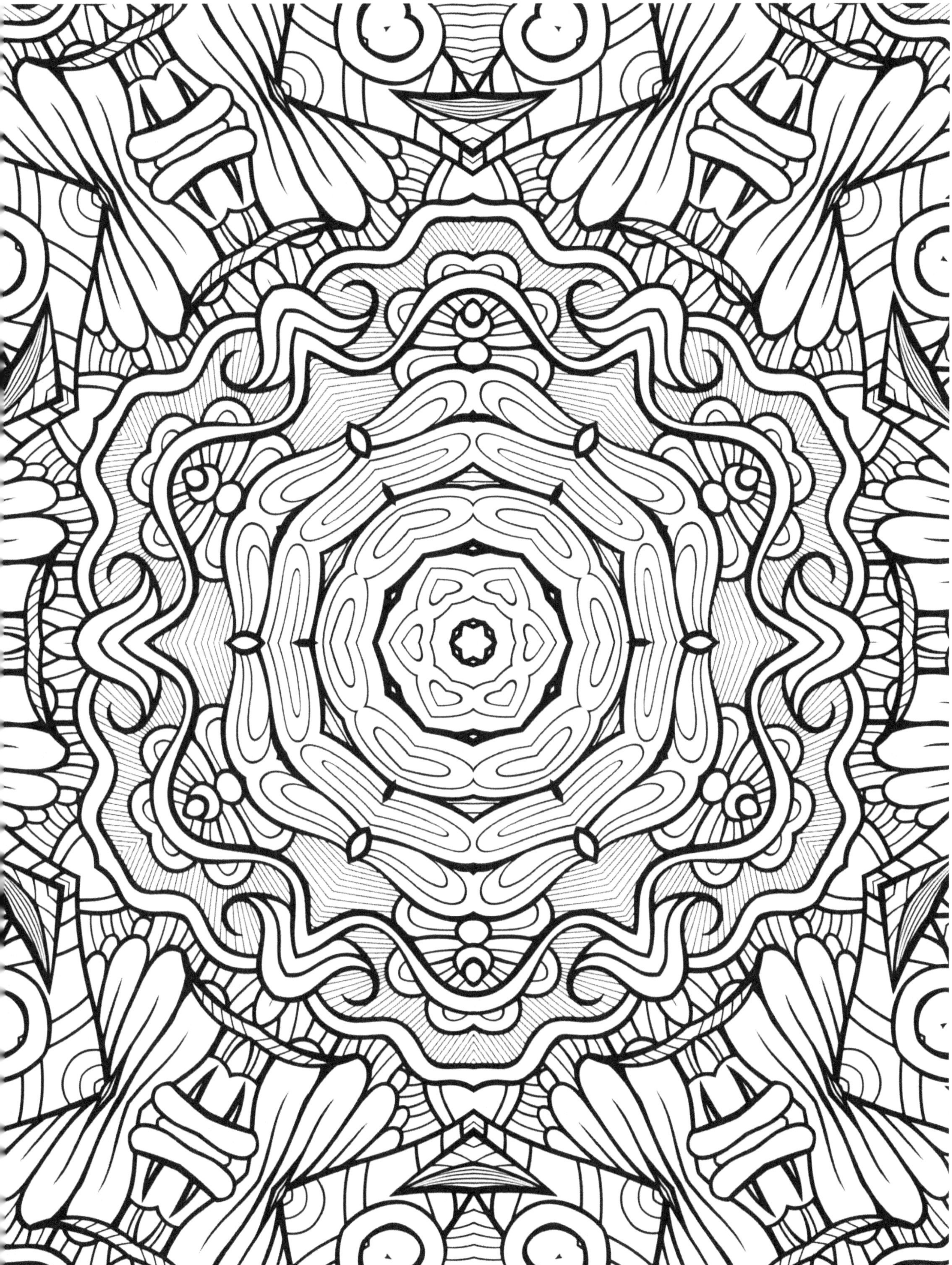

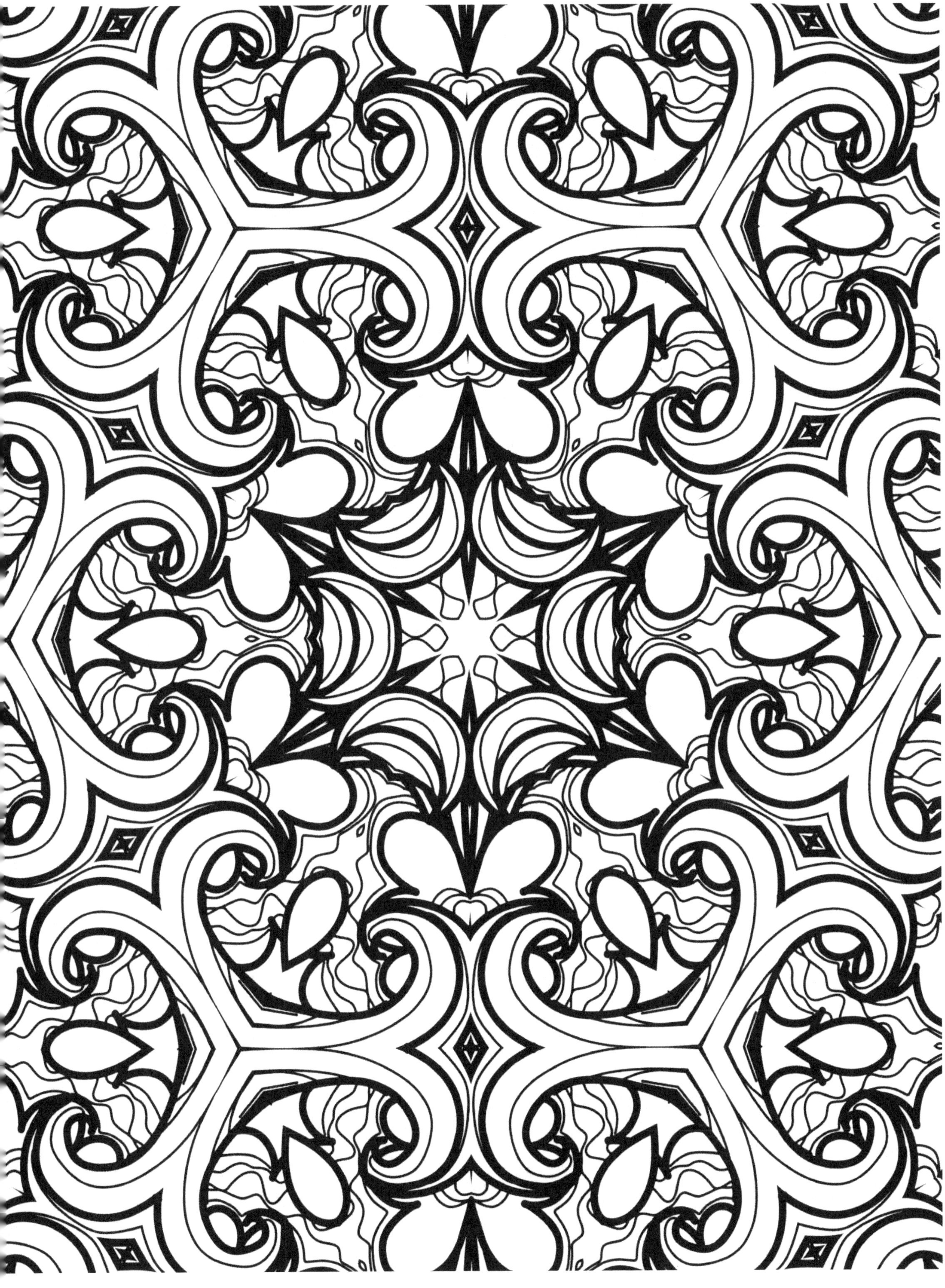

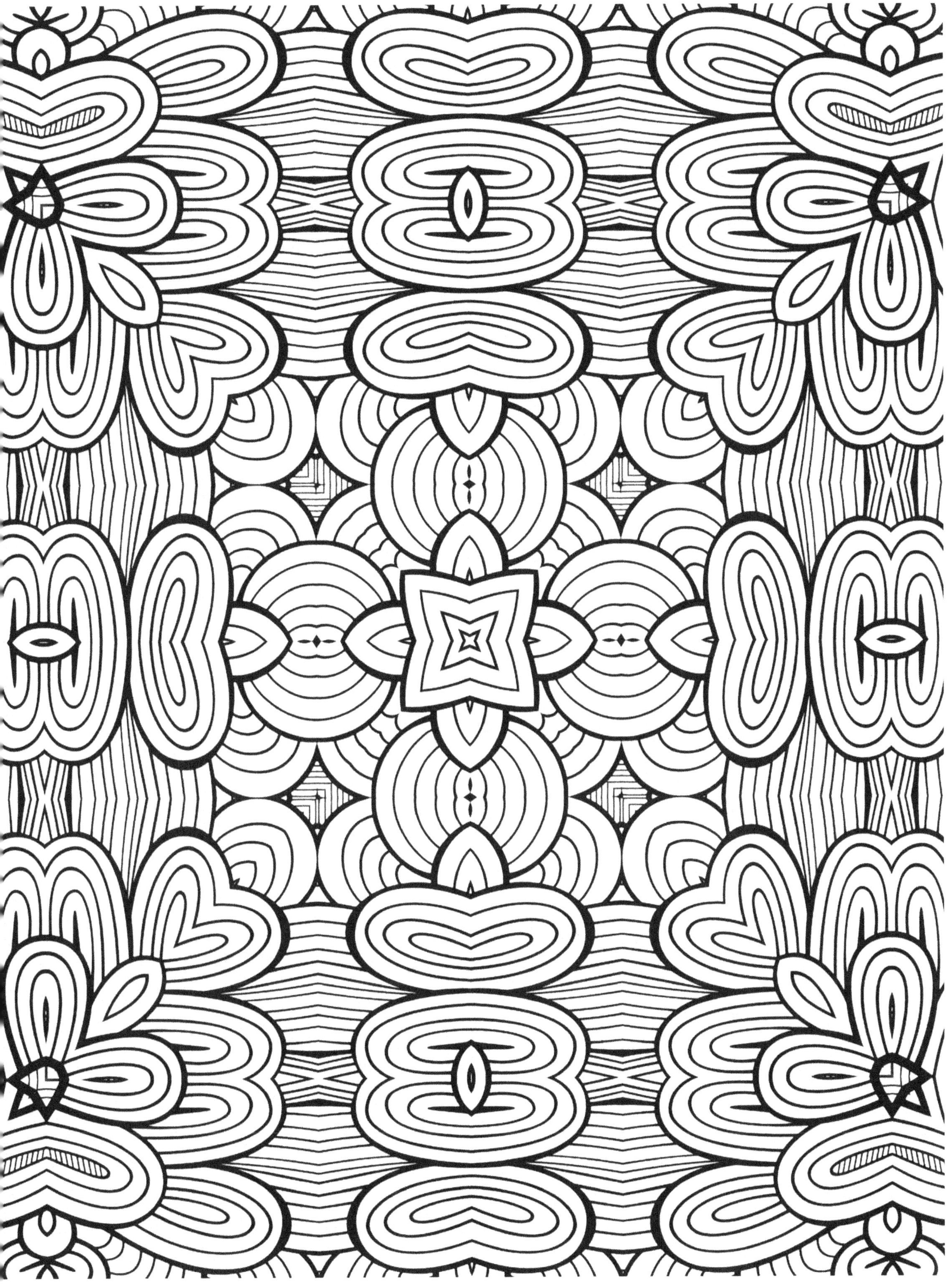

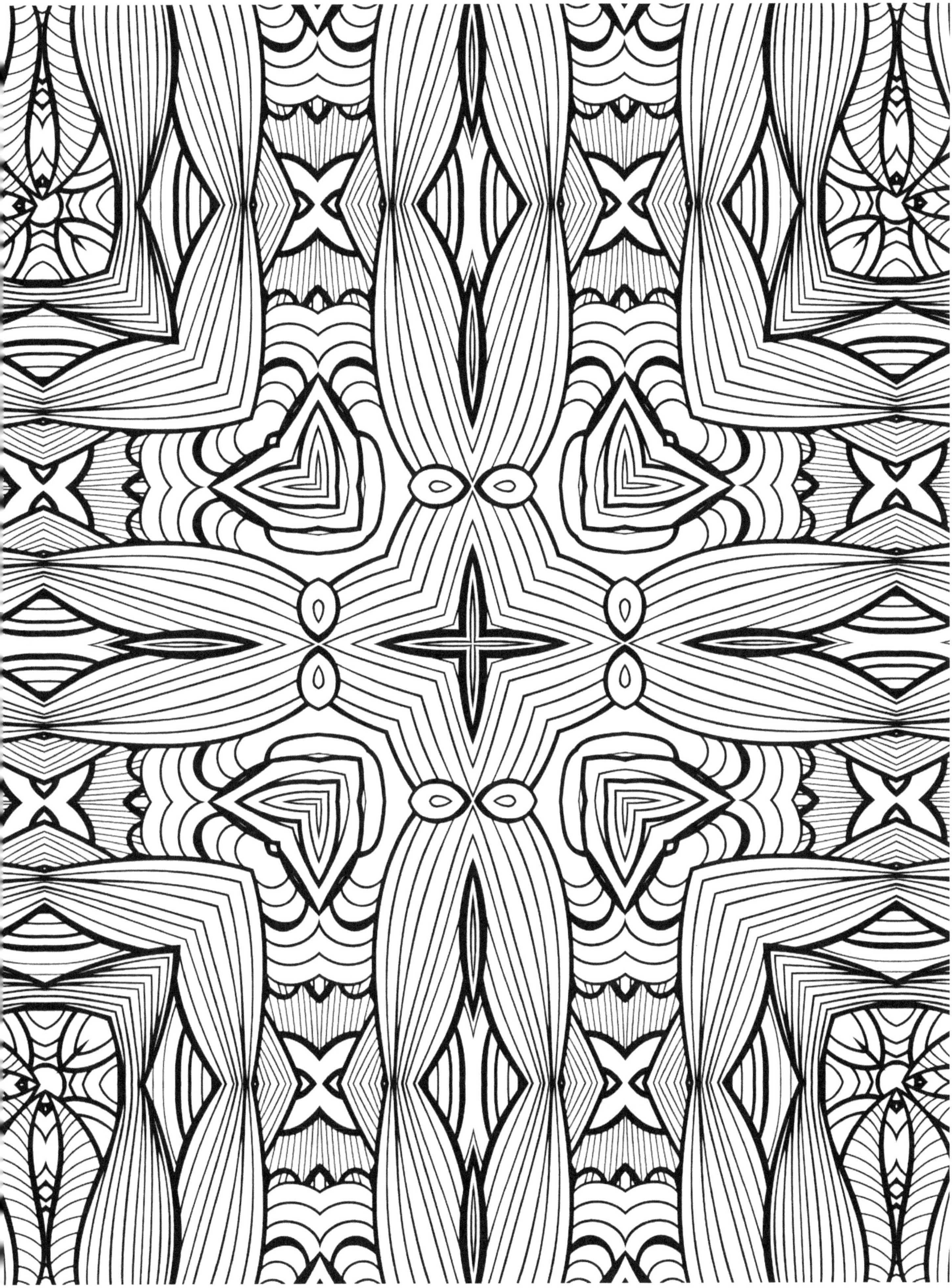

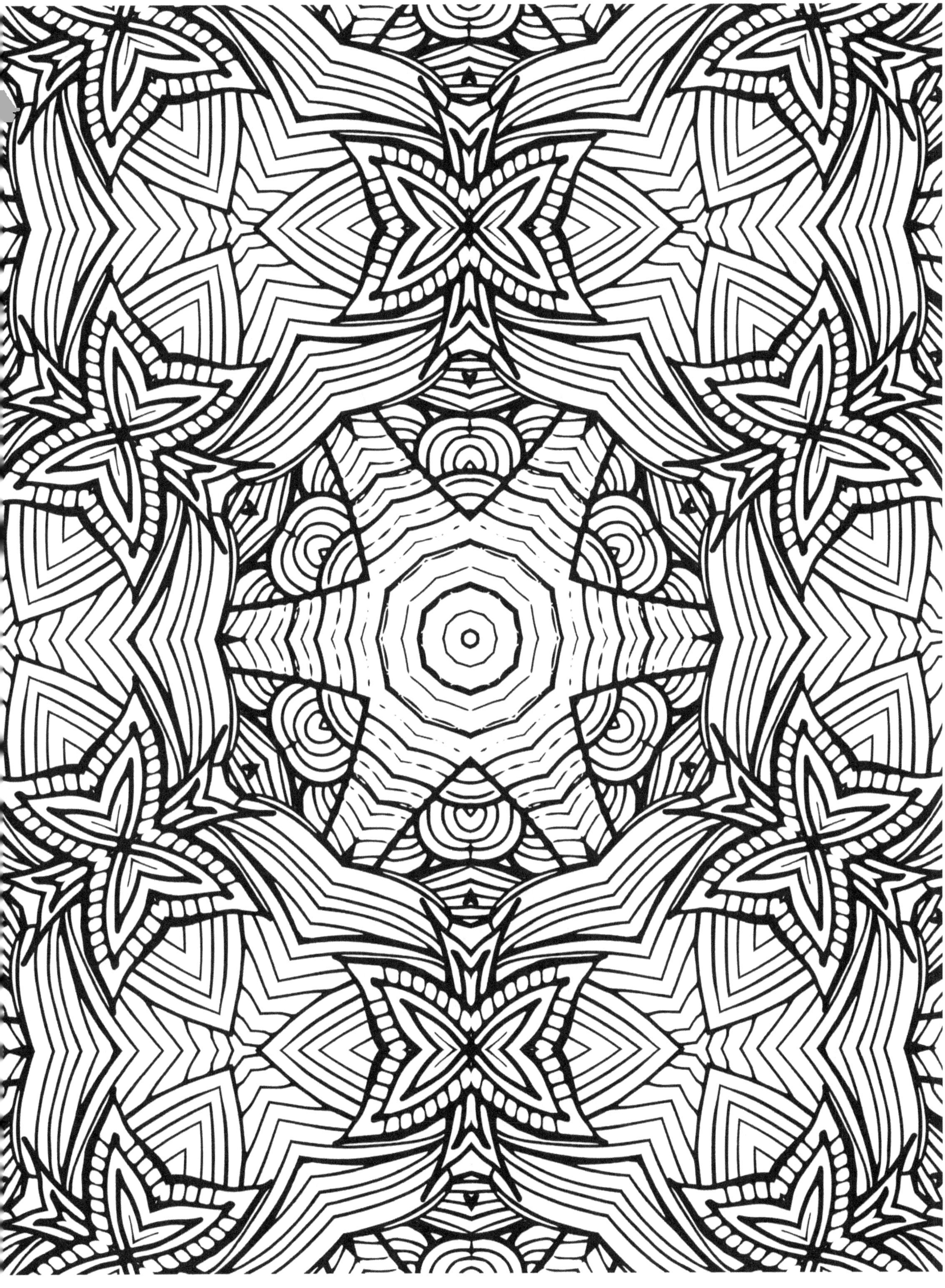

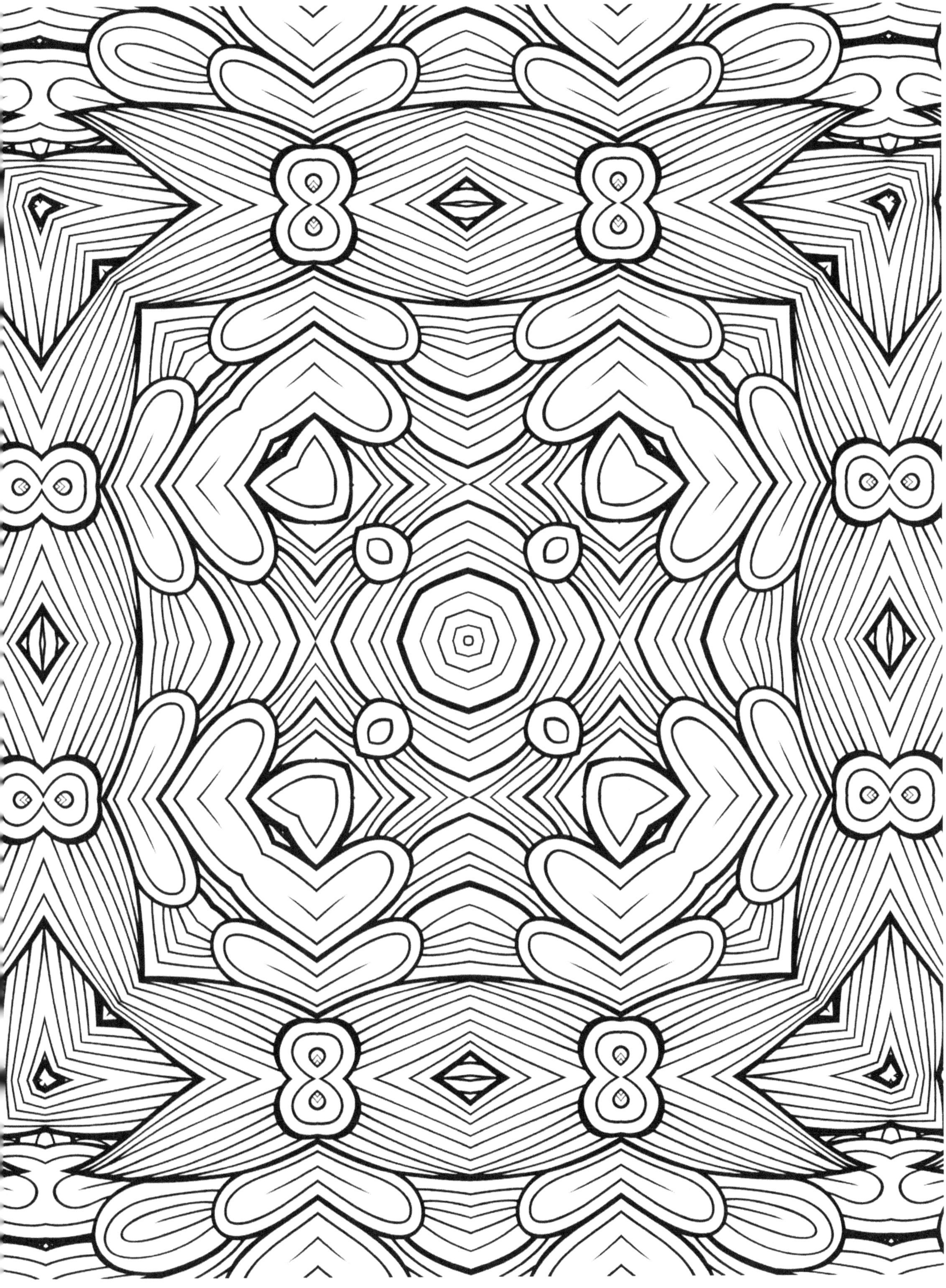

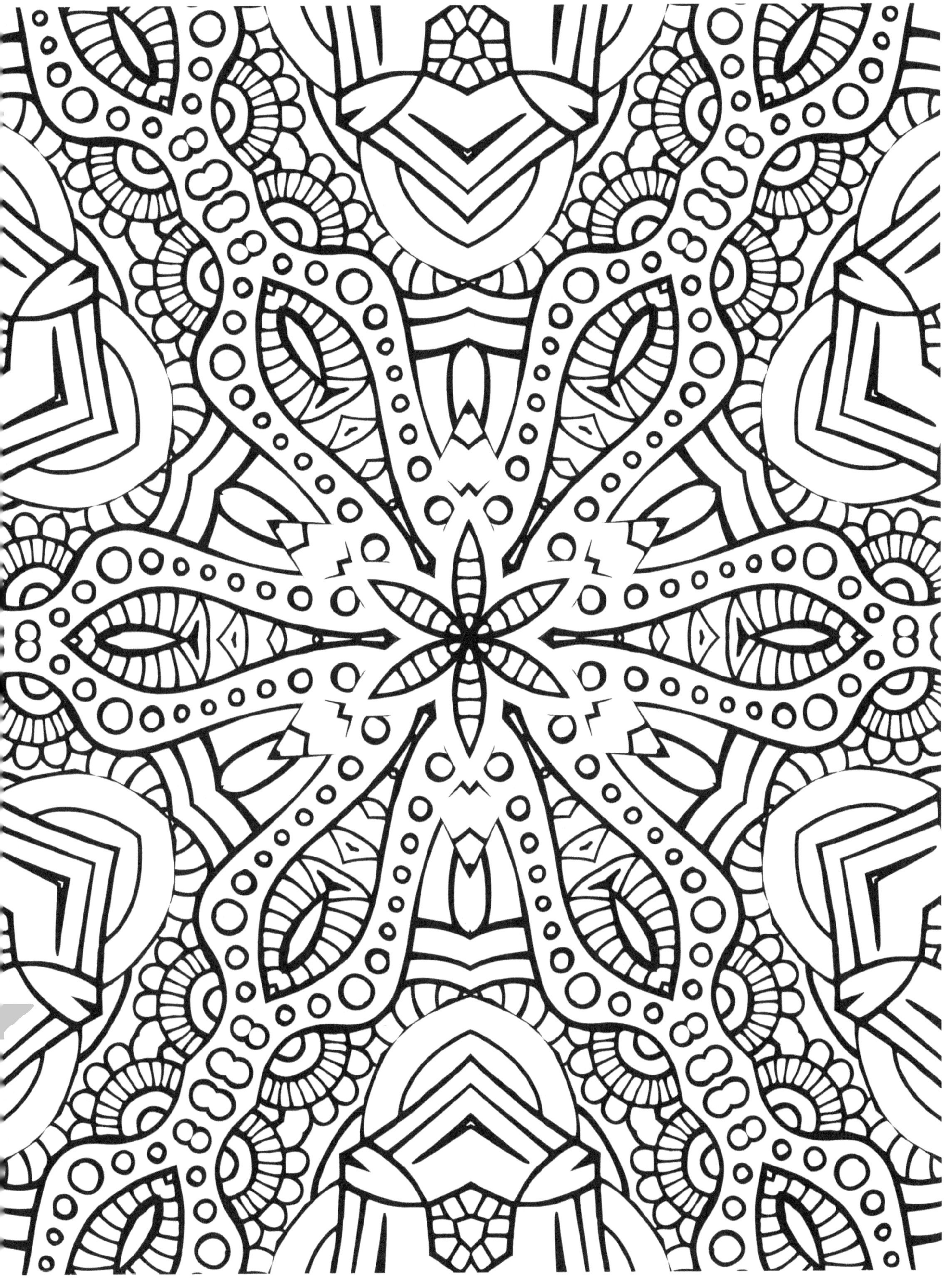

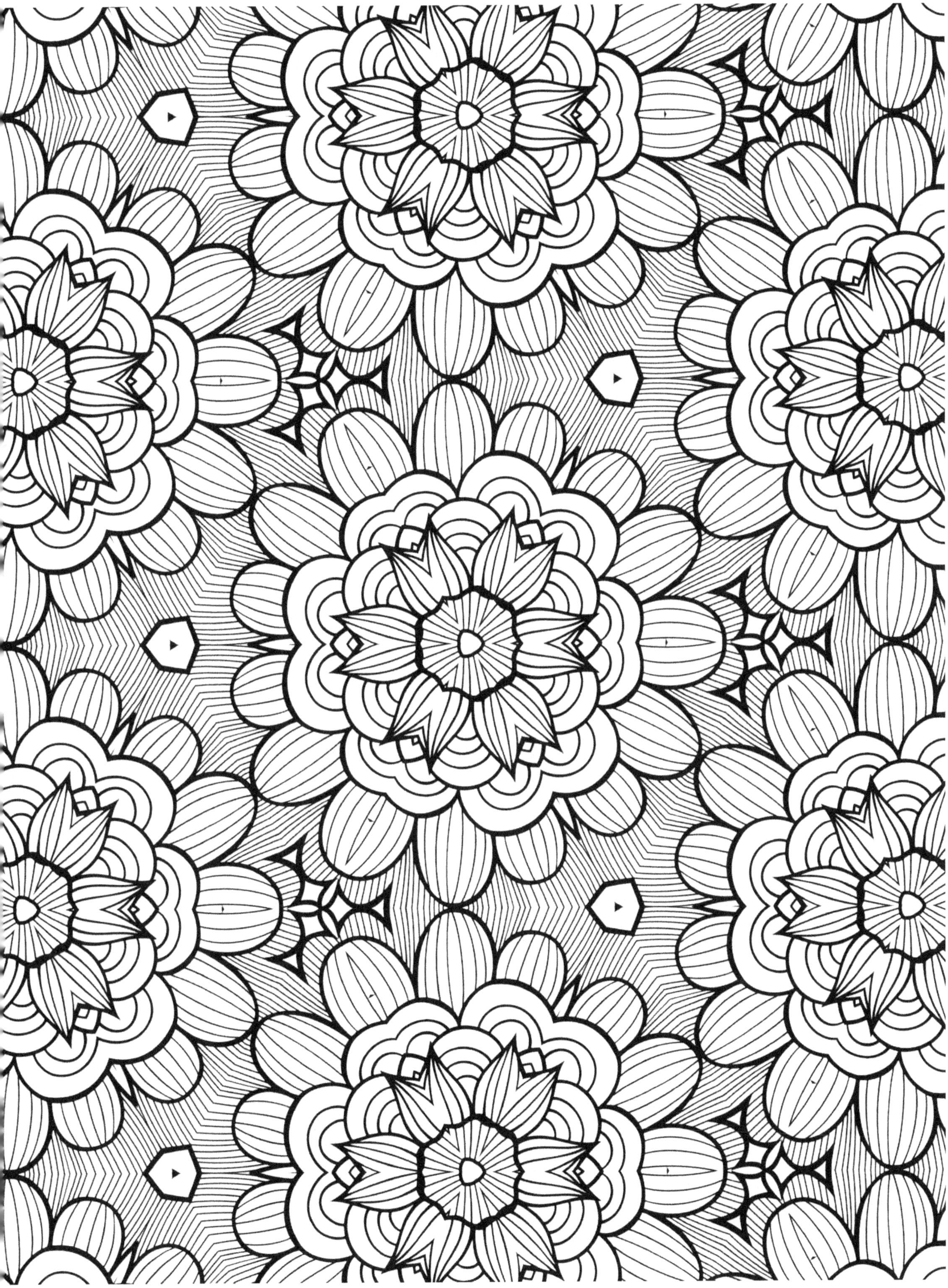

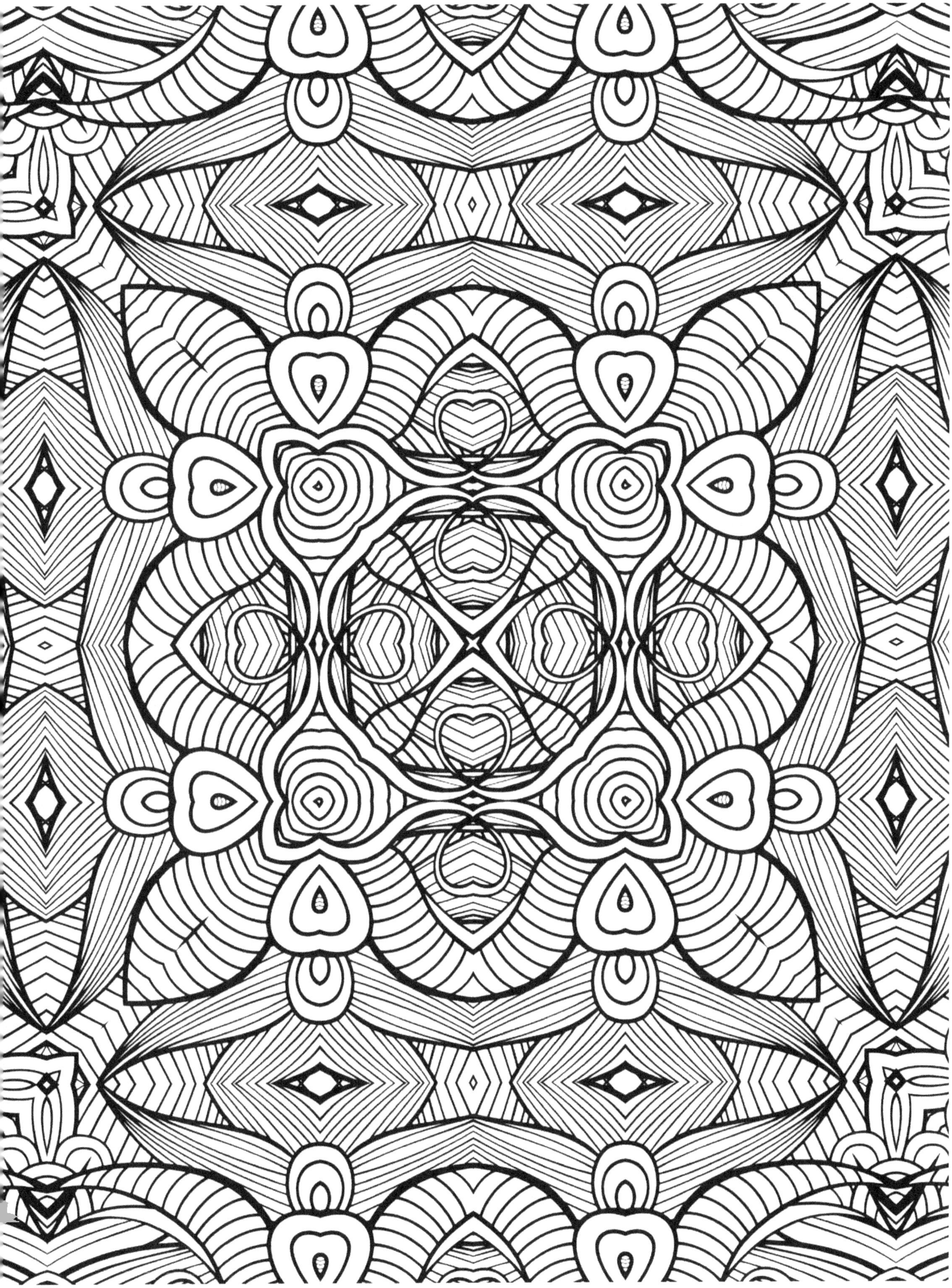

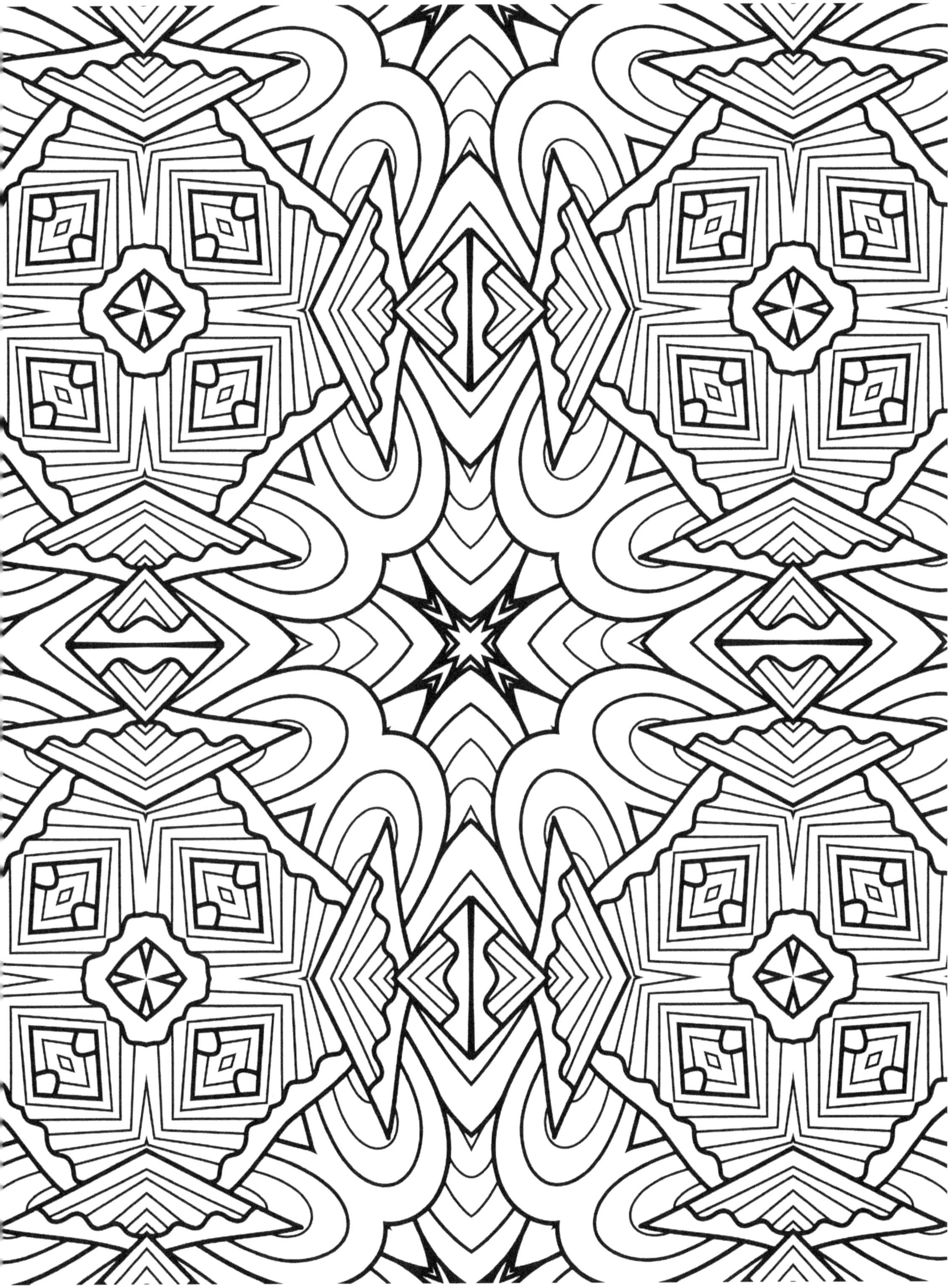

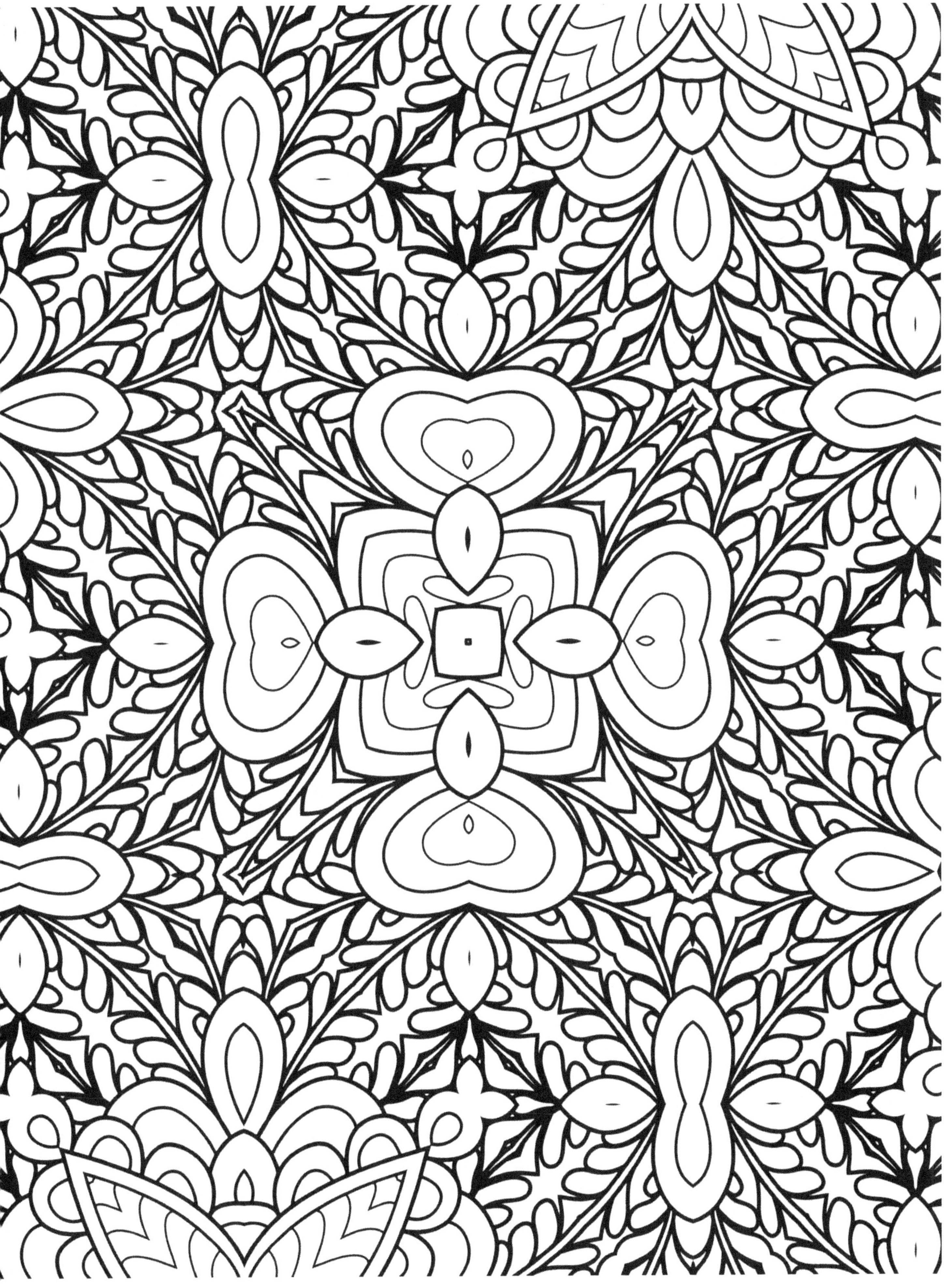

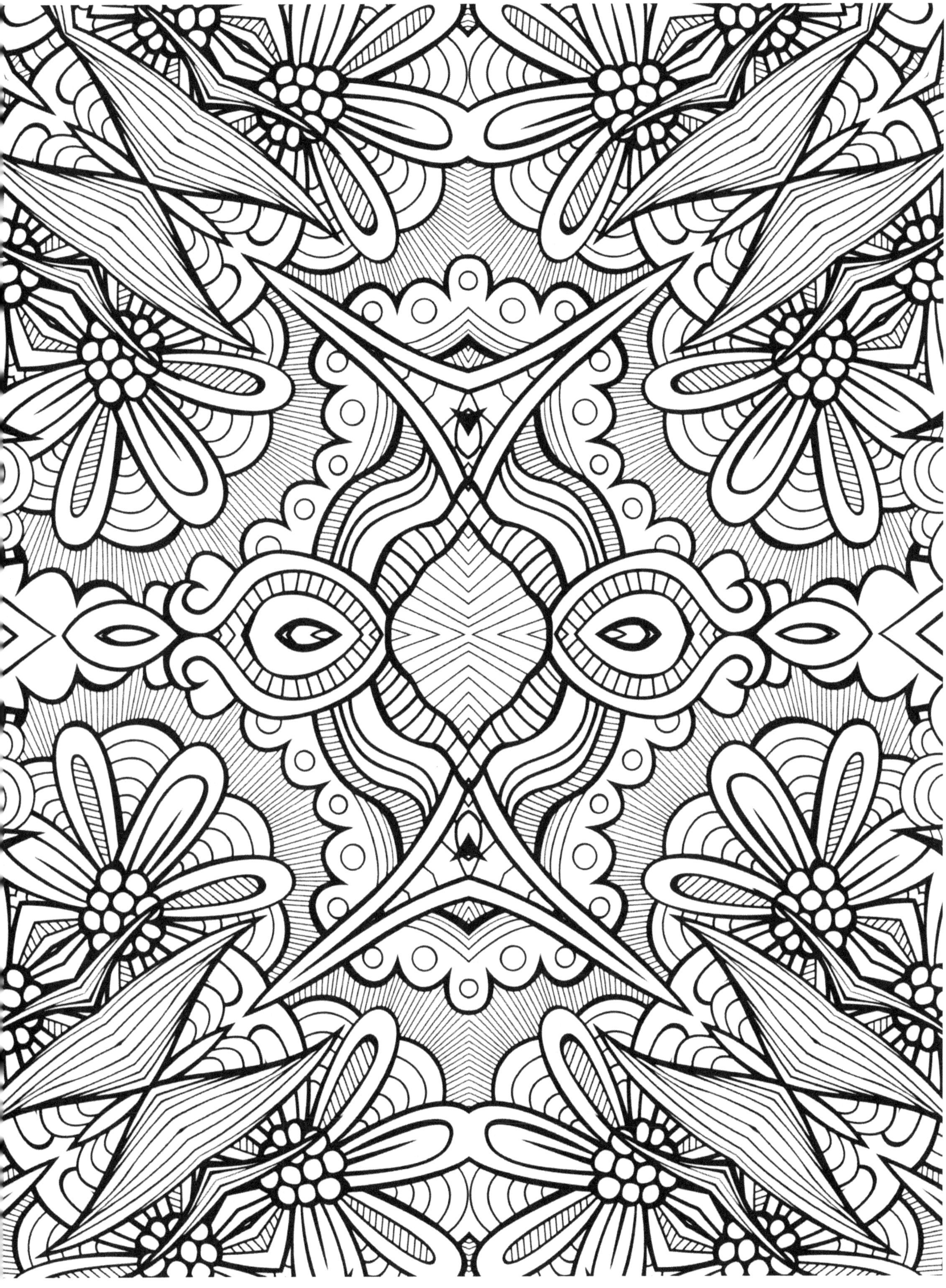

www.ingramcontent.com/pod-product-compliance
Lightning Source LLC
Chambersburg PA
CBHW080509220526
45465CB00006B/2425
* 9 7 9 8 3 7 5 6 5 9 0 2 2 *